Pacifism as Pathology

Reflections on the Role of Armed Struggle in North America

Ward Churchill and Michael Ryan

Pacifism as Pathology: Reflections on the Role of Armed Struggle in North America
Ward Churchill and Michael Ryan
This edition © 2017 PM Press

ISBN: 978–1–62963–224–7
Library of Congress Control Number: 2016948155

Cover by John Yates / www.stealworks.com
Interior design by briandesign

10 9 8 7 6 5 4 3 2 1

PM Press
PO Box 23912
Oakland, CA 94623
www.pmpress.org

Printed in the USA by the Employee Owners of Thomson-Shore in Dexter,
Michigan.
www.thomsonshore.com

For the fallen warriors of the armed struggle,
and for those now in cages.

Contents

Preface to the 1998 Edition

by Ed Mead

> Power grows from the barrel of a gun.
> —Chairman Mao Tse-tung

Okay kids, here we go, my first ever preface to, well, an essay. It displays a kind of logic and research methodology that I myself am not capable of emulating while examining the question of political violence, or, more accurately, the efficacy of adopting a political strategy of nonviolence (pacifism). Pacifism is an important issue for anyone interested in the role of violence in political struggle (a subject one can scarcely ignore in today's world). In my opinion, Ward Churchill has done a good job of addressing the subject. By way of an introduction, then, I will add only a few of my own perspectives. Here goes.

The headline of today's *Seattle Times* screamed, "Experts Warn of Food Crisis Ahead." The story, with graphs showing growing population levels, the limitations of the increasingly depleted soil, and lists of experts and pictures, has probably been long forgotten by most of Seattle's residents. The effects were, after all, presented mostly as being visited upon others elsewhere, the sort of consequence of empire experienced mostly by Third World populations and other equally unimportant groups.

I, too, tend to get pretty mellow about how events are unfolding on the stage of today's world. As a rule, I pay more attention to what is going on here at home, or my attention is focused in the direction the ruling class media pushes me. Like most Americans, I am affected by or in some way understand that there are those who do not, because of their race and nationality, enjoy the many luxuries available to those of us here in the heartland. Twenty years ago, when I was part of Seattle's Prairie Fire Organizing Committee (PFOC), we had a term for those who felt it was necessary and appropriate for people out there in the colonies to fight and die in the struggle against international imperialism while intellectually exempting themselves from incurring the same risks and obligations. The expression used by PFOC back in those days was "American exceptionalism."

I think we can agree that the exploited are everywhere and that they are angry. The question of violence and our own direct experience of it is something we will not be able to avoid when the righteous rage of the oppressed manifests itself in increasingly focused and violent forms. When this time comes, it is likely that white pacifists will be the ruling class's first line of defense. If there is any substance at all to this notion, then we might just as well start the process of having this discussion now instead of later, and that is another reason why I am writing this introduction.

In my opinion, peaceful tactics comprise the only form of political agenda that can be sustained during this particular historical period. Armed actions would not further the struggle for justice at present, but they could plainly hurt it (my reference here is to offensive activities rather than to armed self-defense, which is an altogether different matter, in my view). I suspect that when the situation changes everyone will know it, and the time clearly ain't now.

Anyway, Ward and I reached our respective conclusions about pacifism from different directions. His background is academic, as reflected in the title of his essay, "Pacifism as Pathology: Notes on an American Pseudopraxis." In contrast, I just finished an eighteen-year stretch in prison for having been a part of a political organization that bombed, among other places, the headquarters of the Department of Corrections in Olympia, the Bureau of Indian Affairs building in Everett, and the FBI office in the Tacoma federal courthouse.

I have talked about violence in connection with political struggle for a long time, and I've engaged in it. I see myself as one who incorrectly applied the tool of revolutionary violence during a period when its use was not appropriate. In doing so, my associates and I paid a terrible price. That cost included the loss of comrades Bruce Seidel and Ralph "Poe" Ford. Poe died while planting a pipe bomb in the refrigeration mechanisms located in the back wall of the Safeway store on 15th, and Bruce was killed in a shootout with police at a failed George Jackson Brigade bank robbery. The cost also included the loss to Seattle's progressive movement of many committed militants, who ended up spending many years in various state and federal prisons.

I served nearly two decades behind bars as a result of armed actions conducted by the George Jackson Brigade. During those years, I studied and restudied the mechanics and applicability of both violence and nonviolence to political struggle. I've had plenty of time to learn how to step back and take a look at the larger picture. And, however badly I may represent that picture today, I still find one conclusion inescapable: pacifism as a strategy of achieving social, political, and economic change can only lead to the dead end of liberalism.

Those who denounce the use of political violence as a matter of principle, who advocate nonviolence as a strategy for progress, are wrong. Nonviolence is a tactical question, not a strategic one. The most vicious and violent ruling class in the history of humankind will not give up without a physical fight. Nonviolence as a strategy thus amounts to a form of liberal accommodation and is bound to fail. The question is not *whether* to use violence in the global class struggle to end the rule of international imperialism but only *when* to use it.

By writing in a way that is supportive of the use of revolutionary violence, I want to make it clear that I am not talking about self-destructive avenues like political adventurism. Instead, I am merely objecting to the privileges that pacifists are often able to enjoy at the expense of the global class struggle (one does not see too many pacifists of color these days).

I am not proud of my prison background. At best, I can say that I came out of the prison experience with a bit less damage than many of my peers. But, still, I came out damaged. I don't know how long, if ever, it will take me to really know the depths of that damage. Nonetheless, I managed to do my time in a manner I believe was consistent with communist principles. While I was never the tough guy on the block, and on occasion was seen as a nigger-lovin' commie-fag, I still managed to get by without having to ever snitch on another prisoner or check into protective custody for my own safety. To that extent, I came out okay. But, on the level of having any answers (beyond my limited prison activist's scope), I do not score nearly so well.

With that caveat in mind, what I have to say, and I thank Ward for giving me the opportunity to say it, is this: 99.9 percent of the practitioners of political violence will one day be confronted with imprisonment or death, neither of which is a fun experience. If at some future point we are bound to engage in violent struggle against the government (Gee, why would anyone do that?) it is imperative that we do so in a manner calculated to win. The object is to win.

This is what we thought when the class war was being fought and won around the globe, when somewhere between half a million and a million Americans marched on Washington in 1969, causing H.R. Haldeman to ask President Richard M. Nixon whether this radical event might turn out to be the prelude to a figurative storming of the Winter Palace here in the U.S.A. The television screens of the era, after all, also showed U.S. troops reeling in defeat before Vietnamese liberation forces supplied by both China and the USSR. The same images would shortly be aired with respect to Cambodia and Laos. There were other revolutionary victories in places like Cuba, Nicaragua, Mozambique, and Angola. Substantial guerrilla struggles were being waged at the time in Uruguay, El Salvador, Guatemala, Palestine, Rhodesia, South Africa, the Philippines, and elsewhere. We future Brigade members could see a world in which progressive forces were on the offensive internationally and imperialism was everywhere in retreat.

All we needed to do to bring about final victory, it seemed, was apply pressure on the cracks of empire by opening up fronts in the belly of the beast itself. Thus, some of us on the West Coast began to engage in armed struggle in Los Angeles, San Francisco, Sacramento, Portland, and Seattle. In certain of these places, notably San Francisco, Seattle, and L.A., several groups were doing this work at the same time, and similar units were emerging in major cities across the United States, from Denver to Chicago, from New York to Portland, Maine. We could readily envision a day when all of these seemingly isolated elements would join into one huge fist, battering the whole structure of capitalist oppression to its knees. That was the atmosphere in which the Brigade developed. Conditions seemed genuinely ripe for revolution.

We are nowhere near that situation today, and it must be said that the Brigade was even then premature in initiating armed struggle. We made a grave error, one that was costly in terms of human life and suffering. There is nothing wrong with sacrificing today for a tomorrow that is significantly freer from oppression, but, in our case, the sacrifice did not accomplish the desired political goals. That, I think, was our principle error. However, in spite of all that, as bad as it was, I still tend to feel pride in the fact that we erred on the side of making revolution. If an error is to be made, it seems to me that that's the manner in which it ought to be made.

So, with all of that water under the bridge, you are now presented with the treat of reading Ward's essay on pacifism.

I think you will find that his treatment of the subject is well-reasoned and rational. If you disagree, well, that's your right. But, for myself, I enjoyed the reading. It gave me a solid basis for discussing this topic more intelligently, and that, whatever else might be said, is something all of us need rather urgently at the present time.

All Options: A Reintroduction to *Pacifism as Pathology* in Three Movements

by Dylan Rodríguez

1.

By now, we should be clear that physiological violence is a method of first resort for the modern U.S. state in all its gendered racial mobilizations of official and extralegal power.[1] To enter this conversation, then, is to know that you live under—and may in your own way be accessory to—a terror-inducing racist state, wherein the involuntary inheritances of its vast historical damage are radically asymmetrical, yet the pull of universalizing surrender to the mystified awe of its armed, official, weaponized, and constantly mobilizing power seems gravitational. The common term for this condition of consent, of course, is "patriotism." And therein—within and beyond the symbols, rhetorics, and institutional rituals and protocols of the patriotic American way of life—pulses a national schema that makes an absurdity of pacifism as anything other than an empty dream of moral gratification, utterly and emptily tethered to the moral platitudes and assumptive physical entitlements of white humanity.

Pacifism is the opiate of the white activist world. Not to say that the rest of us are not sometimes seduced by the addictive dream of it as well, but there is little question that foregoing the tools of force—that is, *to reject violent action absolutely and as a matter of moral principle*—is accomplice to the reproduction of the long-running machineries (material, ideological, and paramilitary) of global white supremacy in all its variations. (Respected veteran white Canadian activist Michael Ryan, in his thoughtful follow-up essay to this volume, thus resoundingly affirms that nonviolence "has become a form of catharsis, a practice that allows us to cleanse our souls of the guilt of our white skin privilege for ourselves and for each other without posing a threat either to the state or ourselves." [p. 153]) This is why *Pacifism as Pathology* is a vital text for this historical moment, no less than a tool for dislodging (or at least radically challenging) a stunningly brittle panoply of assumptions about the best possible methods—that is, the most effective, historically impactful, and self-determined praxis—through which systemically targeted peoples might be able to preserve and freely inhabit their bodies and ways of life.

Here, Ward Churchill offers us a layered, historicized, and sensitive response to pacifism that unflinchingly privileges the primacy of radical and liberatory social transformation as a—the—critical ethical imperative for collective political action and insurgent cultural activity. Thus, his critique is not merely a philosophical, theoretical, and political-strategic one, it also reaches toward the theological, the spiritual, the rhetorical, and the therapeutic. To challenge the pacifist position is no less than a confrontation with one of the central methodologies on which a sustainably, oppressively violent global order relies. In these pages, we learn how a thoughtful, critical, radical abolition of pacifism's stranglehold on the political-historical imagination is a comprehensive, complicated task.

My own incomplete extrapolation of the argument that follows: Ward Churchill clarifies how hegemonic (that is, compulsory) pacifism is an entitlement of white social life, a restoration of white supremacist order to the contemporary discourses of progressive social transformation, and an invitation to nonwhite "others" to adjoin themselves to a somewhat horrifying historical tradition of "bearing moral witness" to the programmatic and often indelible disruption

of targeted peoples' ways of being alive, together, autonomous, vulnerable, and often thriving in ways largely illegible
and thus unacceptable to master narratives.

This pacifism—*this* pacifism—is a white position, insuf-
ferable in its moral grandstanding and politically reprehen-
sible in its rejection of other peoples' creative, daring, and
often *violent* approaches to their own always-endangered
practices of human being, enacted against and in spite of
this/our post-Enlightenment and post–civil rights/post-
apartheid/post-colonial humanist order. It is necessary to
come to terms, then, with the damned "pacifist" that haunts
your soul, wherever you are and however you identify. It is
there because white life is a shared curse of the kind that gets
some of us chanting in concert with people who are willing
to tolerate our peculiarly planned obsolescence.

2.

The fundamental contradiction, irreconcilable as it is fatal, is
this: *purely* (that is, dogmatically) nonviolent moral appeals
to state power, when animated by ordinary, vulnerable people's desire to live free of the fear, physiological damage, and
mourning wrought by racist and racist colonial state violence,
actually reproduce the asymmetries of power and suffering
on which the modern Western state form is based. These
asymmetrical relations are not merely a matter of the state's
dominance over military and police power. It is not merely
the racist and violently hetero-patriarchal state's infrastructure of attack against the physical integrity of people's bodies
that incites and inspires insurgency.

The asymmetries are, even more importantly, grounded
in the extra-moral positioning of state violence and the genocidal logic of entitlement through which this position is constantly reproduced. This is to say that even when subjected to
radical (nonviolent) moral challenge, the operative response of
the racist and the racist colonial state is one that unflinchingly
asserts the sanctity of state violence *as* law-and-moral-order.

There is really no such thing as a "moral appeal" to this kind of state, despite the periodic theatrical performances by its representatives and agents that attempt to convey conscience, self-correction, and human fallibility (think President Barack Obama's beer summit, President Bill Clinton's apology for slavery, and the recent handwringing of liberal to conservative officials and pundits, including Attorney General Eric Holder and candidate Hillary Clinton, over the ills, injustices, and inefficiencies of "mass incarceration").

Pacifism is the creeping evidence of deaths foretold, the philosophical residue of selective exterminations ultimately tolerated as tragedy. The morbid, viral theater of twenty-first century, police-directed street tortures against unarmed, ordinary black people as paradigmatic example galvanizes a detectable limit of outrage for those who suspect, maybe somewhere in their recesses, that the brutalized flesh was somehow asking for it. Those and other targeted bodies are only ever destined for pacification—the quelling of a restlessness of being that can only ever be scripted through variations of enforced disintegration. Retaliation, pacifism insists, is simply not an option.

This violence fabricates racial and racial-colonial terror as the fabric of an everyday, historical social form. The terror permeates, constitutes, and ultimately well exceeds (in temporal, spatial, and experiential terms) the state's physical acts of aggression. It insidiously entangles into the political imagination, historical memory, spiritual world, and cultural productions of all who are subjected to its vacillating forces of order/disorder, organization/disruption, threat/protection. This fabric of terror has wrapped itself around the post-1960s "left" position, restraining its political discourse within a default, pathologically pacifist insistence that the only legitimate way to "resist" oppressive conditions is to engage in activist practices that are condoned or sanctioned by the state, and thus more or less guaranteed to *avert the already-present realities of its infrastructures of terror and attack.*

It is no heresy to say that even the most courageous and commendable representatives of strategic nonviolence and principled pacifism have been, at various times, confronted with at least this raw fact of the matter: that the evisceration of their physiological being by an oppressive, persistently violent, and culturally and legally legitimated, oft-celebrated force—whether state or extra-state, police or citizen-mob—may not only be a politically ineffectual sacrifice, but may in fact feed the grist mill of spectatorship on which the oppressive power relies for its reproduction.

Racial colonialism, chattel enslavement, apartheid, military occupation, and neoliberal imperialism are loosely united in their production of *valorized* violence: there is a consistency to their theaters of terror that rests on audacious declarations of necessity, vindication, and the welfare of the civilized world. In other words, the moral high ground on which pacifism relies has often been expropriated and has hence *already "belonged" to the oppressive force*, even and especially as that force executes its protocols of destruction and terror. After the pacifist position recognizes that the politicized ground of moral righteousness has been effectively occupied by the homicidal (if not genocidal) "peacekeeper," then what? At the very least, we are forced to dispose of what Ryan outlines as the "ideological argument" at the heart of nonviolence: that nonviolence is premised on "an alleged moral superiority," and that "if we want to be good . . . we are morally bound to behave in a nonviolent way." (p. 148) What, then, if pacifism facilitates the massive absorption of an oppressive violence that presents itself *as a morally righteous force, executed for the sake of "peace," "safety," and "security"*? Under such conditions of ideological and political antagonism, in which the contest of moral suasion is (even temporarily) won by the dominant regime, it may be the case that pacifism and nonviolence approximate *amoral* or potentially *immoral* positions that neither demystify nor remotely decelerate the machineries of destruction.

3.

Perhaps the issue at hand is not really "morality" or, more specifically, the capacity of masses to convince and cajole the violent state (or extra-state forces) to cease engaging in unjust, oppressive, or otherwise "immoral" operations. As importantly, maybe this is a matter that even reaches beyond the critical acknowledgment that "nonviolence" (or violence) should be framed as a tactical option rather than foundational strategic or ideological commitment. (Recall Professor Churchill's guiding qualification that "it is not being suggested that nonviolent forms of struggle are or should be abandoned, nor that armed struggle should be the normative standard of revolutionary performance." [p. 104]) Maybe the matter is more effectively posed as a deep and principled appreciation of the creative, life-affirming possibilities that are produced in ordinary, seemingly disempowered people's assertions of *radical consequence* against a degrading and toxic social order—actions that may well entail confrontations with state violence that demand a *price be paid* for historical damages rendered.

It is worth considering the possibility that recent—and long historical—revolts against a violent social order are performing something even more than collective demands for justice and freedom, but are also (against their own periodic proto-pacifist rhetorics of protest) breathing dreams of vindicating and avenging violence into and against living, socially activated nightmares, the ugliness of which rests on the constant political-cultural nullification of *the full span* of oppressed peoples' articulations of collective self-defense, self-love, and physiological integrity (liberation).

From another side of this dilemma, then, i wonder if more could muster the will to hold nothing less than contempt and vengeance for the protocols of the national religion (patriotism in its truth) and its pacifist correlate—moreover, to move for a desecration (that is, not merely a disruption or destruction) of the very same personnel, institutions, and cultural structures that compose the central targets of the pacifist's moral and symbolic protest. Of course, it must be reiterated that it is not necessarily the *pacifist* (person) who is the obstruction to (and potential opponent of) the surging collectives desiring radical—and immediate—transformation of an oppressive, human-instituted global order. The obstacle at stake is the central role played by *pacifism* (as ideology, pseudoreligion) in the ongoing mystification of a wretched global arrangement that pivots on the moral denigration, political dismissal, and active repression of resistances, revolts, and proto-revolutionary activities that transcend the prescriptions of nonviolence or "civil disobedience."

Few things are more repulsive than the curtailing of uprising political vistas for the sake of fulfilling the self-righteous moral prescriptions of those who would protect the bodies and lives of the dominant. The truth of the matter is, many of us imagine and dream of violence against our oppressors in vivid, detailed, creative ways. We fantasize the irruption of their worlds, their institutions, their ways of life, *the arrogant presumption of their own permanent, perverse-holy bodily integrity.* Some of us share these thoughts with each other, with humor and candor, as if conspiring toward another kind of peace that sits just on the other side of (their induced, our experienced) terror.

All options are under consideration—they always have been, despite our allegations of self-restraint, civility, and obedience to nonviolent standards. This is the hidden fact of long-running freedom struggles by virtually all peoples whose genealogies include the involuntary and indelibly horrible encounter with the European and white American ascendancy in its Discovery, Civilization, Colonial, Chattel, Imperial, and militarized Neoliberal forms. Some of us see the glimmer of a remade world in their absolute decentering, something wonderful in the demystification of their being by way of nothing other than their full exposure to the earthly, socially fabricated vulnerabilities with which some of us are already intimate—at least, in this way, an awakening of their buried, denied humility through unnatural, externally incited suffering and even death. They will never simply accept this leveling of ground, but to put it another way, there is no other option.

February 2016

Notes

1   Here, "physiology" incorporates the inextricable link between—and thus indicts the overlapping violations of—physical, biological, spiritual, and psychic being, as they converge in the blood, bone, skin, and neural synapses of here and now bodies.

Pacifism as Pathology Revisited
Excavating a Debate (Again)

by Ward Churchill

> We will shoot back.
> —Charles Evers, 1965

It's once again with considerable pleasure, and a certain degree of trepidation, that I (re)introduce my "Pacifism as Pathology: Notes on an American Pseudopraxis," an essay that, I find myself rather astonished to observe, was first published fully thirty years ago. My pleasure of course derives from the extent to which it stimulated what I believe to have been healthy and constructive debate after its initial release in early 1986, a process that has proven to be ongoing, and which seems to be as relevant as ever in the present moment. My trepidation, such as it is, stems from the fact that, as is probably true for the author of anything deemed "controversial" by Those in Charge, or who fancy themselves to be so, I was subjected to a significant amount of ad hominem attack for displaying the temerity of committing to paper what more than a few people were already feeling and in many cases had long been voicing.

Be it said, however, that over the past three decades I've accumulated a wealth of experience with gratuitous smears, both officially sponsored and presumably otherwise.[1] Along the way, I've learned to take the bad (or idiotic) along with the good (and intelligent) in such matters, and to greet the former mostly with yawns, sometimes with chuckles, always with disdain. So, to set things straight right up front, if it makes you feel better "rebutting" the inconvenience of my arguments by whispering that I'm "really" a military intelligence specialist / CIA operative / FBI agent provocateur / SWAT team trainer *cum* new-age hippie ku kluxer with a history of violence against women (among other things, murdering JonBenét Ramsey as part of a plot to overthrow the municipal government of Boulder, Colorado),[2] and a scholarly / ethnic fraud in the bargain,[3] well, have a swell time. And don't forget to include the parts about how the Illuminati put me up to every bit of it, and that—worst of all—I remain an unrepentant smoker of unfiltered Pall Malls. Okay?

For my part, while I could obviously do without yet another round of the backbiting chatter this new edition of *Pacifism as Pathology* will inevitably generate, I was given by my elders to understand from an early age that one is obliged to speak and act in a manner consistent with what one believes to be true, irrespective of pressures or inducements to do otherwise. At every stage of my life, those I've respected have routinely reinforced this principle, usually by example, and I've no intention of discarding it—or, by extension, *them*—at this late date.[4] It follows that I will continue to do as I've always done, saying and writing what I believe to be true, explaining why to the best of my ability, and comporting myself accordingly. This of course includes publishing new editions of my earlier books, perhaps especially those deemed most objectionable by power's myriad suppliants, trusting that in the squalor of their reactions I find validation among those I've termed "the good." For me, the latter are the ones who count.

Backstory

I've been asked to provide a bit of information concerning the essay's origins and evolution into the core of a book with sufficient staying power to be released in a thirtieth anniversary edition. Perhaps obviously, it emerged from the

cumulative frustration attending my years of activist experience from early 1969 onward, as the broadly insurgent movement in which I'd cut my proverbial teeth dissolved into the
(euroamerican) left's generalized "turn to theory,"[5] the "new
age" charade of self-absorbed indulgencies like "est,"[6] and
other such willful diversions, with what remained having
largely harnessed itself to the self-neutralization embodied
in catechistic rituals of "nonviolent protest."[7] As well, and as
a fair number of readers correctly surmised from almost the
moment the essay first appeared in print, there was something much more specific that prompted me to write it.

The incident in question occurred when I accepted an
invitation from Bob Sipe, an organizer of the Midwest Radical
Therapy Association (MRTA),[8] to conduct a workshop at the
group's 1981 annual conference, held near Boone, Iowa.[9] The
premise underlying my session was that many people on the
left displayed an irrational aversion to firearms based upon an
abject ignorance of—and consequent intimidation by—the
technology itself. Worse, they were intent on glossing over
this experiential skills deficiency by proclaiming such weak-
ness to be both a "moral virtue" and a constructive political dynamic.[10] To my mind, and Bob's, this translated into
a posture of deliberate self-disempowerment on the part of
oppositionists, the only possible result of which would be a
virtual monopolization of firepower by the very institutional/
ideological status quo we radicals were supposedly committed to abolishing. To call such practice self-defeating was and
is to dramatically understate the case.

It was our feeling that an antidote to what we perceived
as a psychological logjam might be found in providing
"hands-on" exposure to weapons for those who'd never had an
opportunity to experience it. Our thesis was simple enough:
only by becoming familiar with weapons—to some extent
"demystifying" them—could the psychic baggage preclud-
ing rational decision-making with respect to their potential
utility be stripped away. Embrace or repudiation of the use

of weapons was perhaps a personal choice, we maintained, but in either event the choice needed to be an informed one. Although neither Bob nor I was aware of it at the time, and would've been quite surprised to hear it, ours was in this sense an essentially Gandhian position.[11]

Be that as it may, the workshop I provided—billed as "Demystification of the Assault Rifle"—was well attended, in no small part by a group of lesbian feminists who showed up, as they later acknowledged, mainly to denounce the whole thing as an exercise in "macho swaggering." After a couple of hours spent handling a pair of Heckler & Koch assault rifles—such (at the time) "exotic" weapons were used as a means of heightening the extent to which demystification occurred—learning how and why they're put together the way they are, engaging in Q&A on the applicability of different types of firearms to various situations, and pursuing an altogether calm discussion of the role of arms in a range of political contexts, their perspectives had, as they also acknowledged, been significantly altered. As one of them put it a few days later:

> I still have some very large questions in my mind concerning the appropriateness of armed struggle, and doubt that I'll ever participate in it, but I have to admit that this has changed my outlook on guns and at least *some* of the people who use them. It's going to cause me to look at a lot of things—the Black Panthers, for example—in a whole new way. So, and I'm really surprised to find myself saying this, I think the workshop was really worthwhile and I think we should have more of them in the future. In fact, the instructor offered to come back next a teach people how to actually shoot these things, and I think I'm going to take him up on it.[12]

You'd think, given this sort of favorable response, that similar exercises in demystification/personal empowerment might've been embraced by the MRTA as a whole. Instead, it seems I'd barely left the conference grounds en route back to Colorado before one of RT's leading lights, Claude Steiner, demanded an "emergency plenary meeting."[13] When it was convened that evening, he advanced a resolution for ratification by the membership prohibiting such workshops from ever again being conducted under the organization's auspices and barring anyone from bringing a firearm, whether real or simulated, to a conference for *any* purpose. The quality of the ensuing "discussion" can perhaps be gleaned from Steiner's bald assertion that I was "a killer" who had "absolutely no place in the RT community," and his response, when challenged to muster evidence of my homicidal propensities, that he'd "seen it in [my] eyes."[14]

While laughable on its face, this bizarre "offer of proof" figured integrally in a ruse long used in the political arena to stifle consideration of inconvenient views. As one former new left polemicist explains it, the goal of such exercises is "not to prevail in an argument, but to destroy the enemy's fighting ability"—i.e., their ability to even present a case—by discrediting them personally, thereby "winning the war of ideas" without needing to explain, much less defend, one's own position(s).[15] However crudely, Steiner was merely following a well-established script, shifting the focus of attention from the question at hand to allegations about my "character" and, on that basis, to the proposition that I, together with my "tainted" ideas, should be summarily shunned. As I've learned through countless repetitions, such tactics are no less common in leftist/progressive circles—and, if Bob Black may be taken as an example,[16] those of the anarchist milieu as well—than among those of the reactionary right, academia, or the mainstream media.

Suffice it to say that, although no one who'd actually attended the workshop voted in favor of it, Steiner's resolution was passed by a decisive margin. As if this weren't bad enough, a question was then posed by one of those who'd opposed the measure as to whether, should the cops show up at a future conference, those who'd voted in favor would be prepared to disarm or forcibly eject them. This caused a brief dither before an amendment was quickly mustered and ratified, exempting "police and other civil authorities"—e.g., the FBI—from the MRTA's otherwise blanket ban on weaponry. For at least some of those present, this finally said it all, thoroughly validating a remark I'd made during the workshop Q&A to the effect that, in practice, the term "principled pacifist" can often translated as "active accommodationism," and sometimes as "outright collaborator."[17]

The "controversy" continued to swirl in radical therapy circles for several years. Finally, in mid-1985, Sipe, who'd by then assumed editorship of the RT movement's primary organ, *Issues in Radical Therapy*, asked me to sum up my thinking on the topic for the journal. The result was "Pacifism as Pathology," published in two parts in IRT's winter and spring 1986 issues (Vol. 12, Nos. 1 and 2). By 1987, the piece was being distributed in xerox form by a broad range of radical groups—those were the days before internet—with several hundred copies circulating in Montréal alone. It also served as the basis for a series of intense philosophical/tactical discussions in locales as diverse as New York, Toronto, Chicago, Seattle, Portland, San Francisco, Los Angeles, and Atlanta and was eventually translated into German, French, Spanish, and Arabic.

During the latter, more than a dozen prominent purveyors of the "hegemony of nonviolence,"[18] each of them having pronounced the argument advanced in my essay as absurd (or worse), committed themselves at various times to writing detailed rebuttals for publication. So far as I know, until George Lakey published his twenty-eight-page pamphlet in 2001,[19] none of them ever did so.[20] Nor, as Canadian activist Michael Ryan discovered, were they willing to engage in substantive verbal exchanges. Having spent considerable time preparing to represent "my" side of the argument in a debate set to occur at a radical confab in southern Ontario, he arrived to find that his opponent, locally prominent "peace activist" Ken Hancock,[21] had already arranged to gut the much-anticipated "dialogue" by instigating a brand new "conference rule" limiting each side's presentation to five minutes.

While his experience in this regard was by no means unique, Ryan, provoked by the superficiality thus imposed upon the event, gave rather atypical vent to his frustration by polishing up the draft of a paper upon which he'd intended to base his remarks at the conference and sending the result to IRT. His "On Ward Churchill's 'Pacifism as Pathology'" duly appeared in the Winter–Spring 1988 issue of the journal (Vol. 13, Nos. 1–2),[22] and there things stood for a decade. Then, in 1998, Arbeiter Ring, a start-up press based in Winnipeg, expressed interest in publishing the original essay as a short book. My counterproposal was that Michael's follow-on piece also be included, and that Ed Mead, who'd spent eighteen years in prison for his engagement in armed struggle as a member of Seattle's George Jackson Brigade during the mid-1970s,[23] contribute a brief introduction. This was agreed, with the result that the first edition of *Pacifism as Pathology: Reflections on the Role of Armed Struggle in North America* was released the same year.[24]

Thirty Years On

A lot of water has passed under the bridge since "Pacifism" was originally published. The USSR and Yugoslavia have dissolved, East Germany has been fully (re)absorbed by the West, the entire "Soviet Bloc" of Eastern European countries have gone capitalist, as has China, while both Vietnam and Cuba are trying to follow suit. Nicaragua's Sandinista Revolution has come and gone, as has Hugo Chavez's "Bolivarian" version in Venezuela. Every one of the "Third World socialist states" of Africa, from Algeria to Zimbabwe, has long since collapsed under the weight not only of neocolonialism but also the uniformity of their "revolutionary leaders'" insistence upon emulating Europe's centralized and highly authoritarian modes of governance—i.e., statism itself—rather than seeking alternatives drawn from their own pre-colonial traditions.[25]

Meanwhile, the U.S. has bombed Libya (in two separate air campaigns), Sudan, Afghanistan, the former Yugoslavia, Yemen, Iraq, and a dozen other countries, to say nothing of invading Grenada, Lebanon, Panama, Liberia, Iraq, Haiti, the former Yugoslavia, Somalia, Afghanistan, and Iraq (again).[26] All this is quite apart from the combat missions carried out by the Joint Special Operations Command (JSOC) in well over thirty countries,[27] drone warfare increasingly conducted against targets in at least as many,[28] the use of "irregular" forces as surrogates in Central America, Afghanistan, and elsewhere,[29] the lethal aggressions of U.S. client regimes (notably that of Israel against the Palestinians but also including those of Guatemala, El Salvador, Honduras, Colombia, Bolivia, and Peru against a variety of insurgent forces), and a steadily mounting reliance upon the contracting of merce-nary forces to perform military functions.[30]

As Michael observes in the postscript to his essay, the once promising armed formations in North America and Europe that emerged in response to this sort of imperial aggression during the "Long Sixties" (1958–1975), many of them directly linked to counterparts in the Third World,[31] have long since disappeared from the scene.[32] Indeed, the strongest components in the U.S.—the Black Liberation Army (BLA),[33] American Indian Movement (AIM),[34] and Puerto Rican *independentista* organizations like the Fuerzas Armadas de Liberación Nacional (FALN) and its successor, the Ejército Popular Boricua ("Los Macheteros")[35]—were already largely defunct or greatly diminished by the mid-1980s. Although there were significant armed confrontations between indige-nous activists and the Canadian state at Oka (Mohawk Warrior Society, 1990) and Gustafsen Lake (Ts'peten Defenders, 1995),[36] the mantle of armed struggle has since been carried mainly by ecodefense groups like the Earth Liberation Front (ELF).[37]

As was the case abroad when the U.S. was freed from the cold war era's balance of military power, the veritable disappearance of armed resistance on "the home front" since the mid-1980s, has not led to a diminishment in the state's emphasis upon increasing its capacity to forcibly impose itself. On the contrary, there has been both a dramatic expansion in the number of police personnel and an astonishing "upgrade" in the level of firepower they can now bring to bear and related hardware with which they're equipped. Contrary to the claim fashionable among those of "nonviolent" persuasion—that the vast buildup has a occurred "as a result of 9/11" (read: "terrorist violence")—the fact is that it began twenty years earlier, as part of Reagan's duplicitous "war on drugs," escalated tremendously during the Clinton years, and has undergone by far its greatest surge not under George W. Bush but Barack Obama.[38] As all too many Americans were apparently startled to discover via the images televised by the "news" media during the 2014 confrontations in Ferguson, Missouri, the cops in even smaller U.S. cities can now outgun comparably sized units fielded by most armies.[39]

It's not "just" the police, of course. The legal barrier by which the military sphere was demarcated from the civil, at least in principle, was effectively dissolved by Reagan, resulting not only in militarization of the latter but in active and continues collaboration between the two and the use of special operations units—the Army's Delta Force, to be precise—during the 1987 Atlanta prison revolt, the 1992 ghetto revolt in Los Angeles, the 1999 WTO protests in Seattle, and perhaps elsewhere/more recently.[40] A variation occurred in 2005, when, in the wake of Hurricane Katrina, teams of JSOC-trained mercenaries provided by Blackwater, a primary "military contractor," were dispatched by FEMA to secure key governmental and corporate facilities in New Orleans.[41] Yet another ingredient is the reality that there are now at least as many "private police personnel" in the U.S., most of them weaponized and vested with the same authority as regular cops, as those filling the ranks of the official forces with which they're "partnered."[42]

The attainment of a socially saturating police presence since 1990, corresponded to—and enabled—the wholesale adoption of such "innovative approaches to law enforcement" as "zero tolerance," "stop and frisk," and systematized racial profiling.[43] This dynamic, together with the cops' enjoyment of near blanket immunity from legal consequence,[44] has fostered a virulent contempt for even the most basic rights of those making up the less affluent/privileged sectors of the populace, especially those of other than white complexion. This, in part, explains the monstrous growth of the U.S. prison system over the past thirty years, as well as the marked overrepresentation of people of color among those incarcerated,[45] untold thousands of them as the result of bogus arrests and subsequent "testilying" by the cops.[46]

As one old enough to remember when the Panthers' estimate that, countrywide, the police were murdering a black man, woman, or child at a rate of "one every couple or three days" prompted them to assume a posture of armed self-defense while initiating their hugely popular street patrols to "police the police" in Oakland, I also recall that official violence against black folk in that city sharply declined for several months.[47] A half-century later, during most of which period anything resembling a Panther-style response has been conspicuously absent, the rate of lethal violence inflicted by police upon the black colony has more than doubled, reaching one corpse every twenty-eight hours.[48] Proportionately, more than seven times as many black men aged twenty to thirty-four die at the hands of police as do their white counterparts—for black teenagers, the rate reached a staggering *twenty-one times* as many in 2014[49]—while American Indian men in the same age groups are killed at even higher rates.[50] (Lest I be accused of "sexism" in my framing here, it should be noted that less than 2 percent of *all* those killed by police are female).[51]

The nature of these murders has also undergone a noticeable change. The Panthers first attracted significant public attention in 1967 by exposing the falsity of the official version of how and why a twenty-two-year-old black man named Denzil Dowell had been killed in Richmond, California. Supposedly hit by a single blast from a shotgun while fleeing police after a failed burglary attempt, Dowell, who was unarmed, had in fact been executed by six shots fired at close range from a handgun while standing with his hands raised.[52] Because of the number of rounds pumped into the defenseless victim, the way that his executioners hadn't bothered to summon an ambulance after shooting him, and several other "irregularities," Dowell's death was widely cited at the time as an especially shocking example of police "excess."[53]

Since the 1990s, however, an informal competition has to all appearances taken hold among cops with regard to who can riddle a single human being with the greatest number of bullets: forty-one shots, nineteen of which hit him, were fired virtually point-blank at an unarmed twenty-three-year-old black man, Amadou Diallo, by members of a special New York police unit in 1999;[54] in 2006, members of another special squad in the same city fired fifty rounds, again at close range, into the car of another twenty-three-year-old, Sean Bell, killing him and badly wounding two passengers, all of them black and unarmed;[55] most recently, in Atlanta on August 5, 2016, a U.S. marshal's SWAT team hit twenty-six-year-old black man Jamarion Robinson with an astonishing *seventy-six* rounds, all of them fired at ranges dictated by the interior dimensions of his home.[56]

Under such circumstances, murders like that of the seventeen-year-old black high schooler Laquan McDonald in October 2014 may seem almost benign. McDonald, after all, was shot in the back a "mere" sixteen times for the "offense" of trying to avoid a confrontation with Chicago cops by walking away from them.[57] The more so, victims like

Michael Brown, the black eighteen-year-old shot six times at close range—twice in the head—for allegedly stealing a few cigarillos from a convenience store in Ferguson, Missouri, in August 2014,[58] Walter Scott, the fifty-year-old black man shot five times in the back while fleeing on foot from a North Charleston, South Carolina, cop who'd tased him during a "routine traffic stop" for a faulty taillight in April 2015,[59] or any of thousands of others who've suffered similar fates over the past three decades, the vast majority of them effectively nameless and forgotten.[60] In view of the undeniable persistence of the "trend," the same or worse is all that can be reasonably expected in the years ahead.

There is of course a message embedded in this continuous tone of official, racialized, and gender-specific slaughter, especially in such grotesqueries as the mutilation by gunfire of Jamarion Robinson's corpse,[61] leaving Michael Brown's on display in the middle of the street for four hours,[62] and the refusal of Habersham County, Georgia, authorities to underwrite the medical expenses of then-nineteen-month-old Bounkham Phonesavanh ("Baby Bou Bou"), badly burned and disfigured in May 2014 by a flash-bang grenade tossed into his crib by a SWAT team member amidst a nocturnal drug raid based on false information sworn to by an undercover cop.[63] Most immediately, it amounts to bluntly repetitive (re)statements of the fact that the lives of those inhabiting U.S. internal colonies are valued rather less than swatches of used toilet paper by Those in Charge, a circumstance rendering their individual survival perpetually "contingent" and thereby placing their collective existence on a level elsewhere described as that of "bare life."[64]

This serves to punctuate the broader storyline composed of such earlier-mentioned elements as racial profiling, unremitting psychophysical harassment and brutalization by an ever-more-ubiquitous enforcement apparatus and, to be sure, both the demography and unparalleled scale of the carceral system maintained by "the land of the free." As a whole, the state's ostentatious display of "full spectrum dominance" has as its intended effect to strip those on the receiving end of any real sense of agency—which is to say, the very essence of their humanity—instilling in its stead an utterly disempowering perception that they hold no viable alternative to accepting the degraded status assigned them.[65] In other words, to quote the Borg in Star Trek, the conclusion meant to be drawn is that "resistance is futile."[66]

Notwithstanding unmistakable refinements in its modes of delivery,[67] there's nothing new in any of this. Indeed, while antecedents trace back for centuries, the aggregation of techniques involved have come under the Orwellian heading of "peacekeeping" in the U.S. since 1962, when British counterinsurgency expert Frank Kitson was brought in by the RAND Corporation to impart both the term and its guiding concepts to his North American counterparts.[68] In simplest terms, the idea was and remains that in contexts where unrest has assumed forms destabilizing to the existing order, the most efficient means of averting its potential transformation is by using specialized (para)military units to "surgically eliminate" targeted individuals and organizations—"key activists"—while simultaneously employing a combination of petty concessions and ramped up levels of more generalized repression to "pacify" the discontented mass.[69]

Once the desired state of pacification has been achieved, the resulting "peace"—that is, absence of credible threats to business as usual—is best "kept" by maintaining or incrementally increasing the levels of repressive force suffered by formerly rebellious sectors of the population, especially where it is intended that such concessions as were made for purposes of coopting their revolt be withdrawn, as was the case in the U.S.[70] The process is intensified when, again as in the U.S., it is anticipated by Those in Charge that the conditions which had given rise to widespread rebellion/insurgency would become significantly more acute over the foreseeable future.[71] Propaganda is integral to the process at every step, most concertedly in purported "democracies" like the U.S.,[72] where considerable effort is expended upon concealing the implications attending the ever-more-conspicuous iron fist or the enforcement apparatus within a velvet glove of illusion.[73]

In such contexts, the state, together with collaborating corporations and private foundations, goes to great lengths— including the funding of "oppositional" enterprises like Gene Sharp's Albert Einstein Institution[74]—to convince the oppressed that the remedy to their oppression resides within the oppressive system itself. The means to this end, so the story goes, is for them to "exercise their right to petition the government" while strictly adhering to state-sanctioned tactical constraints, thereby asserting the endlessly touted "freedom" of "speaking truth to power."[75]

What must be understood in appraising the validity of such contentions is that the prescription has never proven successful in context of a police state, and that, contrary to the repetitious forecasts of liberals over the past several decades, the U.S. is in no danger, "if present trends continue," of "becoming" such.[76] Rather, as David Wise and other analysts had concluded by the early 1970s, it already *was* one, and had been so for some time.[77] Since then, Those in Charge have moved far beyond policing in *any* conventional sense as a means of maintaining their position. The entire continuum of methods employed, from counterinsurgency and pacification to peacekeeping, is integral to the modes of "low intensity warfare" taught at the U.S. Army's Special Warfare Center at Fort Bragg, North Carolina, and its so-called School of the Americas at Fort Benning, Georgia.[78]

That being so, any notion that the state's allowing the oppressed to "peacefully protest" their oppression and otherwise "speak truth to power" holds the least likelihood of compelling constructive changes in their circumstances is absurd. At most, as Cherokee activist/artist Jimmie Durham observed more than forty years ago, it boils down to an official guarantee that "people are free to scream under torture."[79] In the worst case, Sharpian "strategies of nonviolence" yield a potential equivalent to Gandhi's 1938 recommendation to "the Jews in Germany to employ *Satyagraha*, the Indian version of passive resistance," as a means of countering and ultimately transforming the racist policies of the nazi state.[80] We all know how well that worked out. No less are we aware of what was actually required to finally bring the nazis to heel.

Why Another Edition?

In light of all this, and much more, the prospect of republishing "Pacifism as Pathology" yet again raises a host of questions for me. Were I starting from scratch today, I'd unquestionably write something rather different, retaining the essential themes and perspectives but with other or additional emphases and examples, couching my arguments in terms wider of the models resulting from its origination in a now largely defunct political landscape. Indeed, I must admit to having sought to do so, at least to some extent, in the preceding section of this introduction. Perhaps I should set out to write a whole new essay, and perhaps at some point I will.[81] Of late, however, whatever urgency I might otherwise have felt in this regard has been diminished by others addressing in depth certain of the topics I've had reason to wish I'd covered more fully.

The work of demythologizing the historic struggle against Jim Crow in the Deep South during the early to mid-1960s has, for instance, been undertaken far more thoroughly—to say nothing of better—than anything I might have offered by Akinyele Umoja in his *We Will Shoot Back*, movement elder Charlie Cobb in his *This Nonviolent Stuff'll Get You Killed*, and others.[82] Similarly, liberal mythologies concerning the Black Panther Party are also being increasingly rejoined and debunked, notably by former Panthers themselves,[83] but also by scholars like Curtis J. Austin and Robin D.G. Kelly.[84] In stark contrast to the recantations and apologies advanced in memoirs published by several of those involved,[85] David

Gilbert's unapologetic *No Surrender*, as well as his autobiographical *Love and Struggle*, do much the same with respect to white anti-imperialists' participation in the armed struggle against U.S. colonialism, as do Leslie James Pickering's *Mad Bomber Melville* and Ed Mead's recent autobiography, *Lumpen*.[86] Hopefully, material of similar quality will soon be available with regard to the American Indian, Puertorriqueño, and Chicano liberation movements "back in the day."

As concerns the current scene, Peter Gelderloos, from his station in "the younger generation" and in his own inimitable fashion, has said much of what I might've said regarding the stultifying stranglehold exerted by proponents purely "peaceful protest,"[87] as, to a lesser extent, has Shon Meckfessel in his *Nonviolence Ain't What It Used to Be*.[88] So, too, Kristian Williams with regard to the police, first in his *Our Enemies in Blue* and then, together with William Munger and Lara Messersmith-Glavin, in the coedited *Life During Wartime*.[89] A number of other examples might be offered, some of them cited in various connections herein.[90] The point, however, is that the issue of tactical diversity has been restored as a focal point of oppositional consideration—and in some circles, practice—to a degree unwitnessed since the second half of the Long Sixties.

The manner in which this growing rejection of tactical straitjacketing might translate into a concrete agenda remains to be seen, but one promising indication may have emerged in the vision statement of the newly established Movement for Black Lives (not to be confused with #Black Lives Matter, from which it in part arose), pronounced by no less jaded a skeptic than Michael Ryan as being "the most comprehensive program I've seen in 30 years."[91] Another is the sustained and very much ongoing blockade physically preventing construction of the Dakota Access Pipeline at a point just north of the Standing Rock Reservation in North Dakota, both as a measure of ecological self-defense and as a substantive (re)assertion of indigenous sovereignty.[92] The level of support rendered by euroamerican radicals in both cases—thus far with no apparent attempt to exert "leadership"—together with the potential for the two movements to in some ways cross-pollinate, becoming increasingly interactive and mutually reinforcing, feels propitious.

Under such circumstances, and given that it contains nothing that I'm inclined to retract, it seems to me that "Pacifism as Pathology" is best left unaltered, serving, as it now does, as a "heritage piece" upon which others have since built and as a tangible link joining the tactical questions posed today with those addressed by my own generation. Especially in the latter regard, it is to be hoped that it yields to younger activists *cum* insurrectionaries the insight that it is unnecessary to figuratively reinvent the wheel in such matters, or at least not in its entirety. That Ryan concurs is fortunate insofar as his follow-on essay not only adds to but in certain respects completes several of my arguments. I've always felt that our two essays work best in tandem.

All that said, thanks are due once again to the incorrigible freedom fighter Ed Mead for his preface and to Dylan Rodríguez for writing the new foreword. I'm honored by both. Thanks also to Ramsey, Craig, Gregory, Jonathan, and the rest of the crew at PM, not only for coming up with the idea of publishing a thirtieth anniversary edition but for seeing it through in such superlative fashion even though my own attention sometimes drifted off in other directions. As for the others to whom gratitude is owed for their support and various contributions over the years, let's just say that while there are far too many to list, you know who you are and how I feel about it.

Notes

1   I say "officially sponsored" both because of my recent and abundantly well-documented experiences with the University of Colorado and the government of that state, and because, as is also documented, I was first targeted by the FBI for COINTELPRO "neutralization" in 1970,

and such operations were apparently continued in collaboration with local police intelligence units until at least as late as the mid-1990s. For documentation, see Barbara Alice Mann, "And Then They Build Monuments to You," the foreword to my *Wielding Words Like Weapons: Selected Essays in Indigenism, 1995–2005* (Oakland: PM Press, 2017).

2   Improbable though it may seem, this is actually the short list of rumors/accusations circulated about me over the years, often by self-styled "progressives" hoping to discredit my views. While the JonBenét conspiracy riff was the work of Cathy Henry, a certifiable right-wing loony—and high school teacher in Arlington, Virginia—who, calling herself "Snapple," peddled it in the blogosphere for several years. Her prattle was invoked by San Francisco State feminist studies instructor Rachel Byrne in her "confidential" effort to prevent my speaking at a 2012 Occupy conference in Oakland because of my alleged "gender violence." The origins of the other ill-fitting jackets mentioned are similarly attributable to specific tailors, arising as they did mostly amidst the bitter AIM splits of the 1980s and '90s and recycled most recently by a subset of a transient phenomenon referring to itself as "the New SDS." Here, props for most spectacular contribution are undoubtedly due to the inimitable "Northern California AIM leader" Carole Standing Elk, who somehow managed to string "new-ager," "hippie," "ku kluxer," and "ethnic fraud" together in a single burst of self-contradictory invective, after admitting that she'd agreed "with almost everything [I'd] said" during a talk I'd just delivered as a fundraiser for Berkeley's KPFA radio in 1994. See generally Faith Attaguile, "Why do you think we call it struggle?" (1998; posted 2010), online at http://kersplebedeb.com/posts/Churchill_struggle-2/.

3   The source of the slurs on my scholarship were unquestionably official. See Don Eron, Suzanne Hudson, and Myron Hulen (Colorado Conference of the American Association of University Professors [AAUP]), "Report on the Termination of Professor Ward Churchill," *Journal of Academic Freedom*, Vol. 3 (2012), online at https://www.aaup.org/JAF3/report-termination-ward-churchill#.WDC7maIrJ1N. On the source(s) of the "ethnic fraud" accusations and related nonsense, see Attaguile, "Why do you think we call it struggle?"; Mann, "And Then They Build Monuments to You."

4   A couple of examples of this are recounted in "Reflections on Gord Hill's *500 Years* and the Nature of Indigenous Resistance," my introduction to Hill's *The 500 Years of Resistance Comic Book* (Vancouver: Arsenal Pulp Press, 2010) pp. 7–20.

5   This might be as aptly described as a "turn *away* from concrete action" or "failure of nerve." While I'd personally date its inception to a

point several years earlier, the period 1975–1980 is generally accepted as that in which it occurred. See Timothy Brennan, *Wars of Position: The Cultural Politics of Left and Right* (New York: Columbia University Press, 2006) pp. ix–xiii; for outcomes, see especially pp. 170–204.

6   For those fortunate enough to have never heard of "est," it stands for "Erhard Seminars Training," a mishmash of, among other things, scientology, gestalt therapy, sensory deprivation, and Synanon cobbled together by "Werner Erhard" (real name, John Paul Rosenberg) during the early 1970s and thereafter peddled as a pricey ticket to "human fulfillment." Quite popular among affluent "counterculturalists" and former—mostly white—participants in the antiwar movement, by mid-decade, it—along with the increasingly wealthy "Erhard"—gradually faded from view. By 1990, however, over a million people had anted up to undergo a weeklong "seminar." The best critique is Sheridan Fenwick's *Getting It: The Psychology of est* (Philadelphia: J.B. Lippincott, 1976). Also see Steven Pressman, *Outrageous Betrayal: The Dark Journey of Werner Erhard from est to Exile* (New York: St. Martin's Press, 1993).

7   This is especially striking in view of the reality that, by 1970, there was a rapidly growing disenchantment among participants with the obvious ineffectuality of even the largest nonviolent protests—e.g., the 1969 Moratorium demonstrations in Washington—in terms of compelling substantive changes in policy. As illustration, see the assessment offered by Moratorium organizer Ken Hurwitz in his *Marching Nowhere* (New York: W. W. Norton, 1971). Nonetheless, it would be fair to say that over the next decade this form of inef-fectuality became the veritable gold standard in "oppositionist" circles. See generally John Lofland, *Polite Protesters: The American Peace Movement of the 1980s* (Syracuse, NY: Syracuse University Press, 1993).

8   The "RT movement," a segment of the so-called Freudian left, is likely another of the period's little-known/remembered phenomena. For those unfamiliar with it, its beginnings and early evolution are covered in Jerome Agel and the Radical Therapist Collective, *The Radical Therapist* (New York: Ballantine Books, 1971), Jerome Agel and the Rough Times Staff, *Rough Times* (New York: Ballantine Books, 1973), and Hogie Wyckoff, ed., *Love, Therapy, and Politics: Issues in Radical Therapy—The First Year* (New York: Grove Press, 1976).

9   I suppose it should be noted that I was never part of the RT move-ment. I had friends—Sipe in particular—who were, however, and was very much in agreement with its opposition to psychiatry, the accommodationist therapeutic paradigms, Skinnerian behavior modification techniques, and scams like "est," as well as with its core principle, i.e., effecting radical change in the existing order is

the only viable means of "healing" the psychic wounds inflicted by that order. I was thus what might be called a willing collaborator on a number of occasions.

10   As I recall, I was particularly piqued at the time by Gene Sharp's arguments to this effect in his *Social Power and Political Freedom* (Boston: Porter Sargent, 1980), although I felt the same with regard to his earlier—and probably more influential—*The Politics of Nonviolent Action*, 3 vols. (Boston: Porter Sargent, 1973).

11   "I advocate training in arms [because] non-violence presupposes the *ability* to strike [emphasis added]," the Mahatma observed, adding that, "Taking life may be a duty," and that, "Even man-slaughter may be necessary in certain cases." See Krishna Kripalani, ed., *All Men Are Brothers: Life and Thoughts of Mahatma Gandhi as Told in His Own Words* (Ahmedabad: Navajivan Publishing House, 1960) pp. 121, 134, 138.

12   "Melissa," interviewed by Bob Sipe. According to Bob, she and the other women in her circle said much the same during the plenary session at which the workshop became a point of heated debate after I left.

13   Steiner, a practitioner of what he called "radical psychiatry," is generally considered to have been a founder of RT, circa 1970. A frequent contributor to the movement quarterly *Issues in Radical Therapy* over the next decade, he'd already begun a transition into more "professionally respectable" realms by 1981. His last article in IRT appeared in 1979; thereafter, his primary venue was the *Transactional Analysis Journal*.

14   The exchange was later recounted to me by several individuals who were present. Allow me to observe that, while as a Vietnam combat vet I may well be guilty as charged, Claude Steiner never had occasion to venture a searching gaze into my eyes. Indeed, he stayed as far from me as was physically possible during the few hours I was at the conference.

15   David Horowitz, *The Art of Political War and Other Radical Pursuits* (Dallas: Spence, 2000) p. 10. For those unaware of his background, long before his current vocation as a shill for the rabid right, Horowitz figured in Berkeley's student dissent during the mid-1960s and later served as an editor of *Ramparts*, one of the left's more influential periodicals until its demise in the mid-1970s. For background, see Peter Richardson, *A Bomb in Every Issue: How the Short, Unruly Life of Ramparts Magazine Changed America* (New York: New Press, 2009).

16   The consistency reflected in Black's lengthy record of relying upon character assassination, often to the extent of outright snitch-jacketing, as an expedient means of "winning" theoretical disputes is truly remarkable. That he is himself a *documented* snitch, yet is still

accorded a certain degree of respect by people who should know better, is even more so. Instructively, his smears are often quite popular on right-wing blogs like Discover the Networks and David Horowitz's FrontPage Magazine. See, e.g., Bob Black, "Up Sand Creek Without a Paddle," FrontPage Magazine (November 2006), now online at http://www.discoverthenetworks.org/Articles/Up%20 Sand%20Creek%20Without%20a%20Paddle2.html. A February 21, 1996, informant letter sent by Black to the Seattle police is posted online at http://www.seesharppress.com/black.html. For an attempt to excuse his conduct, even while acknowledging it, see Anonymous [Aragorn], "In Defense of Bob Black," Anarchist News (September 21, 2015), online at http://anarchistnews.org/content/ defense-bob-black.

17   As if to deliberately turn what was already a travesty into an outright farce, a woman prominent in Steiner's all-white entourage confirmed another of my observations, i.e.: that many of those most insistent in demanding strict adherence to nonviolent methods in the political context were often quick to jettison such principles when "asserting themselves" at a personal level. In this instance, she physically assaulted the sole black man in attendance when he displayed the effrontery of ignoring her order to extinguish his cigarette (he was seated alone at a table on the periphery of what amounted to open-air meeting space). The victim, who wanted to discuss the racial implications of her behavior, was rebuffed by the group, although it was duly noted that the only tangible violence to have occurred during the conference was inflicted by a person on Steiner's side of the dispute.

18   For use of the phrase in quotes (or close variations), as well as solid critiques, see Peter Gelderloos, How Nonviolence Protects the State (Cambridge, MA: South End Press, 2007) p. 1; Ala Alassa, Locating Nonviolence: the people, the past, and resistance in Palestinian political activism (Rice University: PhD dissertation, 2014). Abstract online at https://scholarship.rice.edu/bitstream/handle/1911/76336/ ALAZZEH-THESIS-2014.pdf?sequence=1&isAllowed=y; Rachel Shabi, "Baltimore and the media tyranny of non-violence," Aljazerra News (April 30, 2015), online at http://www.aljazeera. com/indepth/opinion/2015/04/baltimore-media-tyranny- violence-150430070102282.html; Amitai Ben-Abba, "'The Term Has Become Meaningless to Me': On Violence, Social Change, and Nonviolent Communication," Counterpunch (April 15, 2016), online at http://www.counterpunch.org/2016/04/15/the-term-has-become- meaningless-to-me-on-violence-social-change-and-nonviolent- communication/.

19   Although the little screed has long been out of print and is apparently unavailable in electronic form, I'm referring to Lakey's *The Sword That Heals: Challenging Ward Churchill's "Pacifism as Pathology"* (Philadelphia: Training for Change, 2001). It is of course possible that other such rejoinders were printed in local organizational newsletters and circulated in xerox form. If so, however, they've left no trace detectable on the internet. Should any reader happen to be in possession of such a tract, I'd very much appreciate receiving a copy.

20   This isn't to say that a number of writers promoting nonviolence haven't mentioned the essay in passing, or purported to "summarize" the arguments therein, often without appearing to have so much as laid eyes on it. Perhaps the most recent example Karen Kennedy, who, in a single paragraph on p. 54 of her *Deeply Felt: Reflections on Religion and Violence Within the Anarchist Turn* (Raleigh, NC: lulu.com, 2016) changes the title of my "1968 essay" to "pacifism is pathology [emphasis added]"—thereby transforming its meaning—before informing readers that "A K [sic] Press published a second edition of Churchill's book-length work in 2002." The latter might have been true, had it not conveyed the misimpression that my essay comprised the entire book, which it conspicuously didn't (my material, including the intro, encumbers 87 of the 152 pages of text). The *real* howlers begin when Kennedy observes that the 2002 edition was titled *Pacifism and Pathology in the American Left*, the "the same name," she says, as the wrongly dated essay she'd already registered as bearing an inaccurately rendered but nonetheless different title. In actuality, *Pacifism and Pathology* is the title of neither the book nor the essay, but of a spoken word CD. From there, she goes on to "give the activist reader an idea" of the book's "force" by quoting "a large slice" of what she posits as the AK Press collective's "forword." Alas, even were it spelled correctly, the 2002 book has no foreword. Kennedy is in fact quoting from a brief description on the back cover, which also appeared on AK's marketing website. The latter would seem to be the extent of her familiarity with the material she's "summing up."

21   Rather ironically, Hancock's prominence was due in no small part to his having been heavily surveilled and otherwise targeted by the RCMP and Toronto police—"assisted" by both the FBI and CIA—during intensive operations resulting from the 1982 bombing of a Litton facility producing Cruise missile guidance systems outside the city. The action was subsequently attributed to the so-called Vancouver 5 (or Squamish 5)—Ann Hansen, Brent Taylor, Julie Belmas, Doug Stewart, and Gerry Hannah—a group independent of Hancock's Cruise Missile Conversion Project. For background, see Ann Hansen, *Direct Action: Memoirs of an Urban Guerrilla* (Oakland:

AK Press, 2002) pp. 269, 293–352; Hancock's travails on pp. 360–61. Also see "FBI, CIA offer to hunt bombers," *Reading Eagle* (October 17, 1982).

22   IRT was undergoing a transition at the time and ran double numbers from 1988 through '90, in an effort to remain current. The idea was to gradually convert it into a quarterly retitled *New Studies on the Left*, both for purposes of broadening its scope and in homage to *Studies on the Left*, a seminally important new left publication based in Madison, Wisconsin, during the early 1960s. Hence, the journal carried both titles when Ryan's piece appeared. Unfortunately, a combination of several factors—not least the dissolution of the RT movement, and with it most of the subscriber base—led to the journal's being scuttled before it could ever be released under the new title alone.

23   See Daniel Burton-Rose, *Guerrilla USA: The George Jackson Brigade and the Anticapitalist Underground of the 1970s* (Berkeley: University of California Press, 2010) and his edited volume, *Creating a Movement with Teeth: A Documentary History of the George Jackson Brigade* (Oakland: PM Press, 2010).

24   In 2007, AK Press put out a second edition of the book, unchanged apart from a new twenty-eight-page preface by Derrick Jensen. It should be mentioned that, contra Karen Kennedy (see note 20, above), both the title and the subtitle fall under the rubric of "unchanged."

25   These themes are developed at length in my "Unthinking Eurocentrism: The Indigenist Alternative to Marxian 'Anti-Imperialism,'" in Deepa Naik and Trenton Oldfield, eds., *Critical Cities: Ideas, Knowledge and Agitation, Volume 5* (London: Myrdle Court Press, [forthcoming] 2017).

26   For a chronology spanning the period 1986–2003, see my *On the Justice of Roosting Chickens: Reflections on the Consequences of U.S. Imperial Arrogance and Criminality* (Oakland: AK Press, 2003) pp. 74–79.

27   See Jeremy Scahill, *Dirty Wars: The World Is a Battlefield* (New York: Nation Books, 2013).

28   Jeremy Scahill and the Staff of The Intercept, *The Assassination Complex: Inside the Government's Secret Drone Program* (New York: Simon & Schuster, 2016).

29   Specifically at issue here are the U.S.-sponsored contras used against Nicaragua and the Mujahidin in Afghanistan. See generally Holly Sklar, *Washington's War on Nicaragua* (Boston: South End Press, 1999); Bruce Reidel, *What We Won: America's Secret War in Afghanistan, 1979–1989* (Washington, DC: Brookings Institution Press, 2014).

30   Undoubtedly the best-known example is that of Blackwater USA, founded in 1997 by former Navy SEAL *cum* billionaire Erik Prince,

renamed Blackwater Worldwide in 2007, then re-renamed Xe Services in 2009 (after being charged with a variety of criminal offenses), then sold to an "investment group" and re-re-renamed Academi in 2012. Other heavy hitters have included Triple Canopy (now merged with Academi) and DynCorp International, but there are a number of lesser entities. See generally Jeremy Scahill, *Blackwater: The Rise of the World's Largest Mercenary Army* (New York: Nation Books, 2007); P.W. Singer, *Corporate Warriors: The Rise of the Privatized Military Industry* (Ithaca, NY: Cornell University Press, 2003).

31   As Ryan also observes, without going into detail, there were during the 1970s and early 1980s a number of secular Third World organizations like the Popular Front for the Liberation of Palestine (PFLP) with which the European guerrillas in particular could collaborate in the armed struggle against imperialism. Today, these have all but entirely given way to Hamas, Hizbullah, ISIS, Al-Qaeda, and a welter of other Islamist entities for which working alliances with non-Muslims are virtually impossible.

32   By 2006, the last of the major players—the Basque separatist group, Euskadi Ta Askatasuna (ETA)—had declared a ceasefire. Those that had either done the same or dissolved themselves earlier included the Provisional Irish Republican Army (IRA, or "Provos"—ceasefire, 1997); Italy's Brigate Rosse (Red Brigades—dissolved 1988); Germany's Revolutionäre Zellen (Revolutionary Cells—dissolved 1995), Rote Zora (dissolved—1995), and Rote Armee Fraktion (Red Army Faction, or RAF—dissolved 1998). There are, however, indications that some of the Provos resumed combat operations in 2011, one wing of the Red Brigades may never have ended them (albeit, its last known action was in 2003), and former RAF members are the key suspects in a series of audacious armed robberies of armored car money transports in 2015–2016 (these actions are not directly political, instead being actions to secure the livelihood of at least three former RAF members who remain stranded underground).

33   A solid history of the BLA neither exists nor is likely to in the foreseeable future, but see Jalil Muntaqim, *On the Black Liberation Army* (Toronto: Abraham Guillen/Arm the Spirit, 2002) and Akinyele Omowale Umoja, "Repression Breeds Resistance: The Black Liberation Army and the Radical Legacy of the Black Panther Party," in Charles E. Jones, ed., *The Black Panther Party [Reconsidered]* (Baltimore: Black Classics Press, 1998) pp. 417–42.

34   On AIM's period of armed struggle, nothing subsequently published improves upon Peter Matthiessen's *In the Spirit of Crazy Horse* (New York: Viking Press, [2nd ed.] 1991).

35 There is no particularly good history of these groups available in English. The best option remains Ronald Fernandez, *Los Macheteros: The Wells Fargo Robbery and the Violent Struggle for Puerto Rican Independence* (New York: Prentice Hall, 1987).

36 See generally Donna Goodleaf, *Entering the War Zone: A Mohawk Perspective on Resisting Invasions* (Penticton, BC: Theytus Books, 1995) and Janice G.A.E. Switlo, *Gustafsen Lake: Under Siege* (Peachland, BC: TAIC Communications, 1997).

37 See Craig Rosebraugh, *Burning Rage of a Dying Planet: Speaking for the Earth Liberation Front* (Brooklyn: Lantern Books, 2004); Leslie James Pickering, *Earth Liberation Front: 1997–2002* (Binghamton, NY: Arissa Media Group, 2006). On the related Animal Liberation Front (ALF), see Anthony J. Nocella III and Steven Best, *Terrorists or Freedom Fighters? Reflections on the Liberation of Animals* (Brooklyn: Lantern Books, 2004).

38 For a good overview, see Radley Balko, *Rise of the Warrior Cop: The Militarization of America's Police Forces* (New York: PublicAffairs, 2013). Also see Peter B. Kraska, ed., *Militarizing the American Justice System: The Changing Roles of the Armed Forces and the Police* (Boston: Northeastern University Press, 2001).

39 For a sample of "lamestream" media coverage packaged for the previously oblivious, see Taylor Wofford, "How America's Police Became an Army: The 1033 Program," *Newsweek* (August 13, 2014), online at http://www.newsweek.com/how-americas-police-became-army-1033-program-264537. For a cogent analysis, offered more than a decade earlier to those who were paying attention, see Matthew T. DeMichelle and Peter B. Kraska, "Community Policing in Battle Garb: A Paradox or Coherent Strategy?," in Kraska, *Militarizing the American Justice System*, pp. 82–101.

40 Such operations are contextualized in my preface to the South End Classics edition of my and Jim Vander Wall's *The COINTELPRO Papers: Documents from the FBI's Wars Against Dissent in the United States* (Cambridge, MA: South End Press, 2003), especially pp. xliv–liv. Also see Col. Charles J. Dunlap Jr., "The Thin Green Line: The Growing Involvement of Military Forces in Domestic Law Enforcement," in Kraska, *Militarizing the American Justice System*, pp. 29–42.

41 Scahill, *Blackwater*, pp. 321–40. Also see note 30, above.

42 See generally James F. Pastor, *The Privatization of Police in America: An Analysis and Case Study* (Jefferson, NC: McFarland, 2003). For deeper background, see my "The Security Industrial Complex," in Steven Best, Richard Kahn, Anthony J. Nocella II, and Peter McLaren, eds., *The Global Industrial Complex: Systems of Domination* (Lanham, MD: Lexington Books, 2011) pp. 43–96.

43   For a good background survey of effects in the city of origin, see
      Andrea McArdle and Tanya Erzen, eds., *Zero Tolerance: Quality of Life
      and the New Police Brutality in New York City* (New York: NYU Press,
      2001). More broadly—and pointedly—see Kristian Williams, *Our
      Enemies in Blue: Police and Power in America* (Brooklyn: Soft Skull Press,
      2004), especially pp. 244–57.

44   For example, "U.S. government prosecutors have declined to bring
      charges against police officers facing allegations of civil rights viola-
      tions in such cases during the past 10 years"—i.e., "they turned down
      12,703 potential civil rights violations out of 13,233 total complaints
      between 1995 and 2015"—thereby assuring "the officer in the street
      [that s/he] will not be held accountable if [s/he] commit[s] murder or
      other civil rights violations." Walt Peretto, quoted and summarized in
      "U.S. police officers kill with impunity: Researcher," *PressTV* (March 16,
      2016), online at http://www.presstv.com/Detail/2016/03/14/455719/
      Walt-Peretto. It should be noted that even when charges *have* been
      brought, whether at the federal, state, or local level, judges' eviden-
      tiary rulings and grants of defense motions for changes of venue to
      police-friendly locales have precluded convictions in even the most
      egregious/best documented cases. Among the best known examples
      are the 1992 verdict on the beating of Rodney King (Los Angeles), the
      2000 verdict on the murder of Amadou Diallo (New York), and the
      2008 verdict on the murder of Sean Bell (New York).

45   See Marc Mauer, *The Race to Incarcerate* (New York: New Press, [rev.
      ed.] 2006); Michelle Alexander, *The New Jim Crow: Mass Incarceration
      in the Age of Color Blindness* (New York: New Press, 2010), especially
      pp. 95–136.

46   This "routine practice," as San Francisco police commissioner
      publicly described it in 2011, has long been common knowledge
      among prosecutors and judges alike, but nothing has been done
      about it, leading Alan Dershowitz, among others, to charge them
      with complicity in the cops' often blatant perjury and other falsifica-
      tions of evidence. See Alan M. Dershowitz, "Controlling the Cops;
      Accomplices to Perjury," *New York Times* (May 2, 1994), online at
      http://www.nytimes.com/1994/05/02/opinion/controlling-the-cops-
      accomplices-to-perjury.html; Christopher Slobogin, "Testilying:
      Police Perjury and What to Do About It," *University of Colorado Law
      Review*, Vol. 67, No. 3 (Fall 1996) pp. 1037–60, online at http://www.
      constitution.org/lrev/slobogin_testilying.htm; Peter Keane, "Why
      Cops Lie," *SFGate* (March 15, 2011), online at http://www.sfgate.com/
      opinion/openforum/article/Why-cops-lie-2388737.php.

47   Conversation with Bobby Seale and Kathleen Cleaver, September
      28, 2016. On the extent of the party's popularity in the black colony,

circa 1970, as revealed in multiple polls conducted by Lou Harris and others, see Philip S. Foner, ed., *The Black Panthers Speak* (Philadelphia: J.B. Lippincott, 1970) p. xiv.

48   For detailed analysis, see Malcolm X Grassroots Movement [Arlene Eisen], *Operation Ghetto Storm: 2012 Annual Report on the Extrajudicial Killing of 313 Black People by Police, Security Guards and Vigilantes* (April 2013), online at https://mxgm.org/wp-content/uploads/2013/04/Operation-Ghetto-Storm.pdf. The rate is continuing apace in 2016. See Julia Craven, "Here's How Many Black People Have Been Killed by Police This Year [Updated]," *Huffington Post* (October 13, 2016), online at http://www.huffingtonpost.com/entry/black-people-killed-by-police-america_us_577da633e4b0c590f7e7fb17?.

49   On the rate for young black men, see Nicole Flatow, "Black Male Teens Are 21 Times More Likely to Be Killed by Cops Than White Ones," *ThinkProgress* (October 10, 2014), online at https://thinkprogress.org/report-black-male-teens-are-21-times-more-likely-to-be-killed-by-cops-than-white-ones-72fb08a1dbda#.fboxtfbf6.

50   See, e.g., AJ Vicens, "Native Americans Get Shot by Cops at an Astonishing Rate," *Mother Jones* (July 15, 2015), online at http://www.motherjones.com/politics/2015/07/native-americans-getting-shot-police.

51   It's also worth noting that 98 percent of the killer cops are male, and 87.5 percent are white. See Melanie Poole, "When We Talk about Police Shootings, We Need to Talk about Gender," *Feministing* (December 17, 2014), online at http://feministing.com/2014/12/17/when-we-talk-about-police-shootings-we-need-to-talk-about-gender/.

52   See Joshua Bloom and Waldo E. Martin Jr., *Black Against Empire: The History and Politics of the Black Panther Party* (Berkeley: University of California Press, 2013) pp. 50–57.

53   In truth, the only thing truly unique about the nature of Dowell's murder was the manner in which the Panthers' armed response caused it to be publicized. See Bloom and Martin, *Black Against Empire*, pp. 56–58; Curtis J. Austin, *Up Against the Wall: Violence and the Making and Unmaking of the Black Panther Party* (Fayetteville: University of Arkansas Press, 2006) pp. 77–80.

54   See Michael Cooper, "Officers in Bronx Fire 41 Shots, And an Unarmed Man Is Killed," *New York Times* (February 5, 1999), online at http://www.nytimes.com/1999/02/05/nyregion/officers-in-bronx-fire-41-shots-and-an-unarmed-man-is-killed.html; Jane Fritsch, "The Diallo Verdict: The Overview; 4 Officers in Diallo Shooting Are Acquitted of All Charges," *New York Times* (February 26, 2000), online at http://www.nytimes.com/2000/02/26/nyregion/

diallo-verdict-overview-4-officers-diallo-shooting-are-acquitted-
all-charges.html.

55   See William K. Rashbaum and Al Baker, "50 Bullets, 1 Dead, and
Many Questions," *New York Times* (December 11, 2006), online at
http://www.nytimes.com/2006/12/11/nyregion/11shoot.html;
"Officers Acquitted in Sean Bell Case: N.Y. Police Acquittal Sparks
Anger, Appeals for Calm," *Tell Me More* (April 25, 2008), online at
http://www.npr.org/templates/story/story.php?storyId=89938081.
It should be noted that the NYPD has attempted to alter/falsify
the "go to" sources of information on this and several other high
profile police murders. See Kelly Weil, "Edits to Wikipedia pages
on Bell, Garner, Diallo traced to 1 Police Plaza," *Politico* (March 13,
2015), online at http://www.politico.com/states/new-york/city-hall/
story/2015/03/edits-to-wikipedia-pages-on-bell-garner-diallo-
traced-to-1-police-plaza-087652.

56   I saw a fair number of corpses in Vietnam, and *none* were shot up so
badly. The marshals claim that Robinson exchanged gunfire with
them, although they've produced no evidence to that effect, and
it seems rather unlikely since both his hands were shot away by
the initial bursts from their automatic weapons. Moreover, since
several slugs were buried in the floor directly beneath his lifeless
body, it is also clear that at least one of his executioners stood over
him methodically firing bullet after bullet into him after he was
dead. See Mo Barnes, "Police shooting of former CAU student
in Atlanta causes outrage," *Rollingout* (August 15, 2016), online at
http://rollingout.com/2016/08/15/clark-atlanta-university-student-
jamarion-robinson-killed-by-police/.

57   While all of the shots were fired from a range of about ten feet by
a single cop, Jason Van Dyke, all of the at least eight others on the
scene lied about what had happened in an effort to cover for him. So,
too, Chicago police investigators—among other things, by destroying incriminating video evidence—as well as the mayor's and district
attorney's offices, both of which suppressed damning dash-cam
videos for over a year. Van Dyke, against whom twenty complaints
of excessive force, racial taunting, and other misconduct had been
lodged over the years—two of them resulted in cash settlements by
the city, but none in a disciplinary action—was belatedly charged
with first-degree murder in November 2015, the first Chicago cop to
suffer such an indignity in thirty-five years. His trial remains pending.
See Sophia Tareen, "Chicago cops' version of Laquan McDonald
killing at odds with video," *Herald News* (December 5, 2015), online at
http://www.theherald-news.com/2015/12/05/chicago-cops-versions-
of-laquan-mcdonald-killing-at-odds-with-video/aneg9zn/?page=1;

Jeremy Gormer, Annie Sweeney, and Jason Meisner, "Cop in dash-cam video to face murder charge," *Chicago Tribune* (November 23, 2015), online at http://www.chicagotribune.com/news/ct-chicago-cop-shooting-video-laquan-mcdonald-charges-20151123-story.html.

58 This is by far the best-known police murder, not least because the cops opted to greet nonviolent protesters in full military regalia and a corresponding array of weapons and equipment. This, in turn, sparked a not so peaceful reaction in some sectors of the community, thereby commanding saturation coverage by the media. See Julie Makinen, "Michael Brown shooting in Ferguson becomes an international incident," *Los Angeles Times* (August 18, 2014), online at http://www.latimes.com/world/asia/la-fg-ferguson-michael-brown-shooting-world-reaction-20140818-story.html.

59 See John Swaine, "South Carolina shooting witness: victim 'just wanted to get away from the Taser'," *The Guardian* (April 9, 2015), online at https://www.theguardian.com/us-news/2015/apr/08/feidin-santana-bystander-walter-scott-shooting-interview. It should be emphasized that use of tasers by the cops to "compel compliance"—or just for the fun of it—has long since become ubiquitous. While they are officially hyped as being "nonlethal alternatives" to other weapons, in 2015, tasers accounted for at least forty-eight police-inflicted fatalities in the U.S. and have been listed as instruments of torture by the UN since 2007. See "Tasers a form of torture, says UN," *Daily Telegraph* (November 24, 2007), online at http://www.dailytelegraph.com.au/tasers-a-form-of-torture-says-un/story-e6freuz9-1225758523986.

60 For an annotated state-by-state roster of more than 2,000 such victims during the 1990s alone, see *Stolen Lives: Killed by Law Enforcement* (New York/Los Angeles: Anthony Baez Foundation/National Lawyers Guild, 1999).

61 Mutilation of a corpse is a formally recognized violation of the law of war, although in the rare instances in which U.S. personnel have actually been prosecuted for such acts charges have been lodged under Article 94 ("failure to obey an order or regulation") and Article 134 ("conduct of a nature to bring discredit on the armed services") of the Uniform Code of Military Justice (UCMJ), rather than as war crimes per se. See, e.g., U.S. Marine Corps, *War Crimes Investigation MCRP 4 11.8B* (Washington, DC: Dept. of the Navy, 22 June 1998), Chap. 1 § 4–5. Online at https://archive.org/stream/War_Crimes_Investigation_MCRP_4-11.8B/War_Crimes_Investigation_ MCRP_4-11.8B _djvu.txt.

62 Julie Bosman and Joseph Goldstein, "Timeline for a Body: 4 Hours in the Middle of a Ferguson Street," *New York Times* (August 23, 2014),

online at http://www.nytimes.com/2014/08/24/us/michael-brown-a-bodys-timeline-4-hours-on-a-ferguson-street.html?smid=pl-share/.

63   The charges, involving the supposed sale of a very small amount of meth to a police informant, were in any case petty. Moreover, the alleged dealer neither resided in nor was present at the raided home. For his part, the obviously unoffending Baby Bou Bou, who suffered extensive "facial burns, a detached nose, brain injuries and a collapsed lung" when the flash-bang detonated only inches from his face, had to be placed in an induced coma until his injured lung could be repaired, then undergo a whole series of reconstructive surgeries. By October, his medical bills were over $1 million and mounting, but the county commissioners held that paying any part of them would be "illegal." And, of course, while a grand jury concluded that their actions were "hurried, sloppy, and unfortunately not in accordance with best practices and policies," none of the raiders was indicted. A federal grand jury did, however, later indict the undercover cop who'd obtained the warrant with false information. Her trial is pending. See "County will not pay medical bills for toddler hurt in Habersham raid," WBS-TV 2 Atlanta (August 15, 2014), online at http://www.wsbtv.com/news/local/lawyer-county-refuses-pay-medical-bills-toddler-hu/137524203; Patrick Frye, "Georgia SWAT Team That Disfigured Baby Bou Bou's Face with a Flash Grenade Will Not Be Charged," Inquisitr (October 7, 2014), online at http://www.inquisitr.com/1524103/georgia-swat-team-that-disfigured-baby-boo-boos-face-with-a-flash-grenade-will-not-be-charged/; "Ex-deputy charged in Habersham raid that injured toddler," Fox 5 Atlanta News (July 22, 2015), online at http://www.fox5atlanta.com/news/4613049-story.

64   On the dynamics of contingency in this regard, see, e.g., Elana Gomel, Bloodscripts: Writing the Violent Subject (Columbus: Ohio State University Press, 2003) pp. xxiv–xxvi. On the other term in quotes, see Giorgio Agamben, Homo Sacer: Sovereign Power and Bare Life (Stanford, CA: Stanford University Press, 1998), especially pp. 136–42.

65   The condition is fundamentally that which was so brilliantly analyzed by Albert Memmi in The Colonizer and the Colonized (New York: Orion Press, 1965).

66   The complete rendering is, "We are the Borg. Lower your shields and surrender your [weapons]. We will add your biological and technological distinctiveness to our own. Your culture will adapt to service us. Resistance is futile." Star Trek: First Contact (Paramount, 1996).

67   One major area of development that has gone unmentioned is that of surveillance technology and attendant infrastructure. In this connection, see Tim Shorrock, Spies for Hire: The Secret World of

Intelligence Outsourcing (New York: Simon and Schuster, 2008) and Ivan Greenberg, *Surveillance in America: Critical Analysis of the FBI, 1920 to the Present* (Lanham, MD: Lexington Books, 2012), especially pp. 269–326.

68 Kitson made his proverbial bones in 1955 as a junior officer developing/applying counterinsurgency techniques against the Mau Mau in Kenya and was promoted to the rank of major as a result of his performance against Malayan insurgents in 1957. By the time of his RAND session, his 1960 book, *Gangs and Counter-gangs*, was already considered a classic in the emerging counterinsurgent literature. In 1970–71, as a brigadier general, he commanded the so-called Military Reaction Force, a "legalized death squad" targeting the IRA in Ulster. See Simon Cursey, "Exposed: The army black ops unit ordered to murder IRA's top 'players,'" *Daily Mail* (November 16, 2013), online at http://www.dailymail.co.uk/news/article-2508511/ Exposed-The-army-black-ops-squad-ordered-murder-IRAs-players. html; "Frank Kitson in Northern Ireland and the 'British way' of counterinsurgency," *History Ireland*, Vol. 22, No. 1 (January/February 2014), available online at http://www.dailymail.co.uk/news/article-2508511/Exposed-The-army-black-ops-squad-ordered-murder-IRAs-players.html. Those inclined to dismiss Kitson's ideas as "outdated" should note that RAND, having recently republished its 158-page report on the proceedings in which Kitson was featured, plainly disagrees. See Stephen T. Hosmer and Sybille O. Crane, *Counterinsurgency: A Symposium, April 16–20, 1962* (Santa Monica, CA: RAND Corp., 2006), online at http://www.rand.org/content/dam/ rand/pubs/reports/2006/R412-1.pdf.

69 One of those taking Kitson's concepts to heart was Col. Louis O. Giuffrida, who set about adapting them to the U.S. domestic context in a thesis titled *National Survival—Racial Imperative*, written during at stint at the U.S. Army War College in 1970, online at https://pdf. yt/d/h7zSh86fNBKrtRJU. Among other things he suggested therein was that during an "exigency," "ghetto[s might] perhaps be cordoned off [as] concentration camp[s]," or that, alternatively, "the evacuation and detention of all blacks from actual or potential trouble spots" could be undertaken by the military in cooperation with law enforcement agencies and "patriotic" citizens' groups. On the strength of this prescription, then California governor Ronald Reagan hired Giuffrida to direct the state's newly formed Special Training Institute (CSTI) in 1971, preparing relevant personnel to implement various aspects of the overall plan. In his new capacity, Giuffrida prepared a series of "counterinsurgency scenarios," two of which, codenamed "Garden Plot" and "Cable Splicer," were apparently field-tested by the FBI during its operations against AIM on the

Pine Ridge Reservation between 1973 and '76. In 1981, after Reagan's election as president, he appointed Giuffrida to direct FEMA, a position he used to fully federalize his "vision" (it is now integrated into the broader planning of the Department of Homeland Security). See Tim Butz, "Garden Plot—Flowers of Evil," *Akwesasne Notes*, Vol. 7, No. 5 (Early Winter, 1975) p. 6; Tim Butz, "Garden Plot & SWAT: U.S. Police as New Action Army," *CounterSpy*, Vol. 2, No. 4 (Winter 1976) pp. 16–24, online at http://jfk.hood.edu/Collection/Weisberg%20Subject%20Index%20Files/F%20Disk/Fifth%20Estate/Item%2007.pdf; Matthew Cunningham-Cook, "Contingency Plans: In a never before released thesis, Reagan's FEMA director discussed the internment of millions of blacks in concentration camps," *Jacobin Magazine* (September 11, 2014), online at https://www.jacobinmag.com/2014/09/contingency-plans/.

70 While the insurgencies of the Long Sixties precipitated a cluster of social and political concessions—notably the 1964 and '68 Civil Rights Acts and the 1965 Voting Rights Act—together with noticeable improvements in the material conditions experienced by elite sectors of the black and indigenous colonies, by the early 1980s the implied promise that this "lift" would gradually extend to the broader populations had evaporated, and their situations "in some respects grew worse." The same pertained over the longer term with regard to political gains, most glaringly with the Supreme Court's effective repeal of the Voting Rights Act through its 2013 opinion in *Shelby County v. Holder*. On material conditions, see Manning Marable, *Race, Reform and Rebellion: The Second Reconstruction in Black America, 1945–1982* (Jackson: University Press of Mississippi, 1984) pp. 168–79; Ronald L. Trosper, "American Indian Poverty on Reservations," in Gary D. Sandefur, Ronald R. Rindfuss, and Barney Cohen, eds., *Changing Numbers, Changing Needs: American Indian Demography and Public Health* (Washington, DC: National Academy Press, 1996) pp. 173–75. On *Shelby County v. Holder*, see Adam Liptak, "Supreme Court Invalidates Key Part of Voting Rights Act," *New York Times* (June 25, 2013), available online at http://www.nytimes.com/2013/06/26/us/supreme-court-ruling.html?_r=0.

71 While Occupy and similar groups have emphasized the stunning disparity of income—reflected in Barack Obama's 2014 observation that the average U.S. employee now "needs to work more than a month to earn what the CEO earns in an hour"—that has increasingly distinguished "the 1%" from "the rest of us" since 1980, this masks the issue of racially defined disparities of wealth *within* the latter. The median wealth of a black family in the U.S. is presently about 1.5 percent that of a white family (as compared to roughly 5

percent in 1975, and 7 percent in apartheid South Africa). Latino family wealth is only marginally better, while several Asian American populations have even less than black folk, and, as always, reservation-based American Indians are the most impoverished of all. See William Marsden, "Obama's State of the Union speech will be call to arms on the wealth gap," *O Canada.com* (January 26, 2014), online at http://o.canada.com/news/obamas-state-of-the-union-speech-will-be-call-to-arms-on-wealth-gap; Antonio Moore, "Our Real Wealth Gap Story: Over 50 years after Martin Luther King Jr.'s March on Washington, median white family has 70 times more wealth than typical black families," *Inequality.org* (January 22, 2016), online at http://inequality.org/racial-wealth-gap-worse-thought/; Lillian D. Singh and Karishma Shamdasani, "The Asian American Wealth Gap: Too Often Ignored," *Huffington Post* (August 8, 2016), online at http://www.huffingtonpost.com/lillian-d-singh/the-asian-american-wealth_b_11395484.html; Ojibwa, "Indians 101: Reservation Poverty," *Daily Kos* (December 6, 2012), online at http://www.dailykos.com/story/2012/12/6/1167663/-Indians-101-Reservation-Poverty.

72   For background, see Robin Evelegh, *Peace-Keeping in a Democratic Society: The Lessons of Northern Ireland* (London: C. Hurst, 1978).

73   The phrase "iron fist in a velvet glove" is loosely attributable to Napoleon. It has, however, been used to describe the U.S. enforcement apparatus since at least as early as the mid-1970s. See Center for Research on Criminal Justice, *The Iron Fist and the Velvet Glove: An Analysis of the U.S. Police* (Berkeley: Center for Research on Criminal Justice, 1975). On propaganda techniques, see Noam Chomsky, *Necessary Illusions: Thought Control in Democratic Societies* (Boston: South End Press, 1989), especially pp. 1–20.

74   In view of his carefully cultivated image as an "antimilitarist," Sharp's relationship to the military—and to established power more generally—has always been curious, to say the least (e.g., his doctoral research was funded in part by the Department of Defense). Among his institution's underwriters have been "the Ford Foundation, the International Republican Institute, and the National Foundation for Democracy (the latter two funded by the US government)." Peter Gelderloos, *The Failure of Nonviolence* (Seattle: Left Bank Books, 2015) p. 179.

75   See Sharp, *The Politics of Nonviolent Action*, especially Vol. 2, *The Methods of Nonviolent Action*. Also see his *Waging Nonviolent Struggle: 20th Century Practice and 21st Century Potential* (Boston: Porter Sargent, 2005).

76   I've heard this refrain from self-described civil libertarians since the late 1960s. At every step along the way, whatever they were arguing "must be prevented" lest "we find ourselves in a police state" has

in fact happened, at which point they've simply moved the goal-posts and repeated the process. Obviously, at some point along the line, what they were warning would come came, yet we continue to hear repetitions of the same stale formulation. As examples of the forecast's persistence, see Richard Harris, *Justice: The Crisis of Law, Order, and Freedom in America* (New York: E.P. Dutton, 1970); Bertram Gross, *Friendly Fascism: The New Face of Power in America* (New York: M. Evans, 1980), especially p. 246; James X. Dempsey and David Cole, *Terrorism and the Constitution: Sacrificing Civil Liberties in the Name of National Security* (Los Angeles: First Amendment Foundation, 1999); William Kunstler and Michael Ratner, *The Emerging Police State: Resisting Illegitimate Authority* (New York: Ocean Press, 2004). As contemporary samples, see Sal Gentile, "Are we becoming a police state? Five things that have civil liberties advocates nervous," *The Daily Need* (December 7, 2011), online at http://www.pbs.org/wnet/need-to-know/the-daily-need/are-we-becoming-a-police-state-five-things-that-have-civil-liberties-advocates-nervous/12563/; L. Michael Hager, "Path to Autocracy: Could America Become a Police State?," *Truthout* (September 22, 2013), online at http://www.truth-out.org/news/item/18802-path-to-autocracy-could-america-become-a-police-state; Lloyd Grove, "Is America Becoming a Police State? The Emerging Implications of 'Do Not Resist,'" *The Daily Beast* (September 30, 2016), online at http://www.thedailybeast.com/articles/2016/09/30/is-america-becoming-a-police-state-the-disturbing-questions-of-do-not-resist.html.

77   See David Wise, *The American Police State: The Government Against the People* (New York: Random House, 1976). Also see Cooper et al., *Iron Fist/Velvet Glove* (a revised and expanded edition was published in 1977, and, with a somewhat different authorial line-up, yet another was published by the Institute for the Study of Labor and Economic Crisis in 1982).

78   See Frank Kitson, *Low Intensity Operations: Subversion, Insurgency and Peacekeeping* (London: Faber and Faber, 1971); Michael Klare and Peter Kornbluh, *Low Intensity Warfare: Counterinsurgency, Proinsurgency, and Antiterrorism in the Eighties* (New York: Pantheon Books, 1987); Deane Searle, *Low Intensity Conflict: Contemporary Approaches and Strategic Thinking* (Saarbrücken: VDM Verlag, 2008). Also see the material cited in note 69, and Ron Ridenhour with Arthur Lubow, "Bringing the War Home," *New Times* (November 28, 1975), now collected in Tom Burghardt, ed., *Police State America: U.S. Military "Civil Disturbance" Planning* (Toronto/Montreal/San Francisco: Arm the Spirit, 2002) pp. 15–26. Credit for first making the Kitson connection should probably go to Ken Lawrence in his *The New State Repression*

(Chicago: International Network Against the New State Repression, 1985).

79   Jimmie Durham, *Columbus Day: Poems, Drawings and Stories about American Indian Life and Death in the Nineteen-Seventies* (Minneapolis: West End Press, 1983) p. 103.

80   Lucy Dawidowicz, *The War Against the Jews, 1933–45* (London: Seth Press, [2nd ed., rev.] 1986) p. 274.

81   In a sense, I've been doing this all along, mainly by integrating the perspectives and arguments at issue into other materials I've written. For a recent example, see my "The Other Kind: On the Integrity, Consistency, and Humanity of Jalil Abdul Muntaqim," a lengthy afterword to Jalil's *Escaping the Prism . . . Fade to Black: Poetry and Essays by Jalil Muntaqim* (Montreal: Kersplebedeb, 2015) pp. 183–293.

82   Akinyele Omowale Umoja, *We Will Shoot Back: Armed Resistance in the Mississippi Freedom Movement* (New York: New York University Press, 2013); Charles E. Cobb Jr., *This Nonviolent Stuff'll Get You Killed: How Guns Made the Civil Rights Movement Possible* (New York: Basic Books, 2014). Also see Timothy Tyson, *Radio Free Dixie: Robert F. Williams and the Roots of Black Power* (Chapel Hill: University of North Carolina Press, 1999); Lance Hill, *The Deacons for Defense and Justice: Armed Resistance in the Civil Rights Movement* (Chapel Hill: University of North Carolina Press, 2006).

83   As examples of such material published since 2000, see the contributions of Mumia Abu-Jamal, Kathleen Neal Cleaver, Geronimo ji Jaga (Pratt), Donald Cox, and Russell ("Maroon") Shoatz in Kathleen Cleaver and George Katsiaficas, eds., *Liberation, Imagination, and the Black Panther Party* (New York: Routledge, 2001); Kuwasi Balagoon, *A Soldier's Story: Writings by a Revolutionary New Afrikan Anarchist* (Montreal: Solidarity, 2001); Jalil Muntaqim, *We Are Our Own Liberators: Selected Prison Writings* (Montreal/Toronto: Abraham Guillen Press/Arm the Spirit, 2002); Nuh Washington, *All Power to the People* (Montreal/Toronto: Solidarity/Arm the Spirit, 2002); Mumia Abu-Jamal, *We Want Freedom: A Life in the Black Panther Party* (Cambridge, MA: South End Press, 2004); Safiya Bukhari, *The War Before: The True Story of Becoming a Black Panther, Keeping the Faith in Prison, and Fighting for Those Left Behind* (New York: Feminist Press at CUNY, 2010); Marshall "Eddie" Conway and Dominique Stevenson, *Marshall Law: The Life and Times of a Baltimore Black Panther* (Oakland: AK Press, 2011); Russell Shoatz, *Maroon the Implacable: The Collected Writings of Russell Maroon Shoats* (Oakland: PM Press, 2013).

84   See Austin, *Up Against the Wall*; Robin D.G. Kelly, *Freedom Dreams: The Black Radical Imagination* (Boston: Beacon Press, 2002). Also see Bloom and Martin, *Black Against Empire*.

85   Two of the worst in this regard are Cathy Wilkerson's *Flying Close to the Sun: My Life and Times as a Weatherman* (New York: Seven Stories Press, 2007) and Mark Rudd's *Underground: My Days with SDS and the Weathermen* (New York: William Morrow, 2009).

86   David Gilbert, *No Surrender: writings from an anti-imperialist political prisoner* (Montreal/Toronto: Abraham Guillen Press/Arm the Spirit, 2004) and *Love and Struggle: My Life in SDS, the Weather Underground, and Beyond* (Oakland: PM Press, 2012); Leslie James Pickering, *Mad Bomber Melville* (Portland, OR: Arissa Media Group, 2007); Ed Mead, *Lumpen: The Autobiography of Ed Mead* (Montreal: Kersplebedeb, 2015). More problematically, albeit in very different ways, see Bill Ayers, *Fugitive Days* (Boston: Beacon Press, 2001) and Susan Rosenberg, *An American Radical: A Political Prisoner in My Own Country* (New York: Citadel Press, 2011). Daniel Burton-Rose's earlier cited *Guerrilla USA* and *Creating a Movement with Teeth* offer exemplary contextualization of Mead's group, while Dan Berger's *Outlaws of America: The Weather Underground and the Politics of Solidarity* (Oakland: AK Press, 2005) makes a valiant effort to do the same with the organization of which Gilbert, Ayers, and—for a while—Rosenberg were part.

87   See Gelderloos's earlier-cited *How Nonviolence Protects the State* and *The Failure of Nonviolence*.

88   Shon Meckfessel, *Nonviolence Ain't What It Used to Be: Unarmed Insurrection and the Rhetoric of Resistance* (Chico, CA: AK Press, 2016).

89   See Williams, *Our Enemies in Blue*, and Kristian Williams, William Munger, and Lara Messersmith-Glavin, eds., *Life During Wartime: Resisting Counterinsurgency* (Oakland: AK Press, 2013).

90   As examples of material already cited, see Rosebraugh, *Burning Rage*; Pickering, *Earth Liberation Front*; Nocella and Best, *Terrorists or Freedom Fighters?* Among the substantial number that haven't been are Derrick Jensen's *Endgame: Volume II, Resistance* (New York: Seven Stories Press, 2006) and scott crow's *Black Flags and Windmills: Hope, Anarchy, and the Common Ground Collective* (Oakland: PM Press, 2011).

91   Movement for Black Lives, *A Vision for Black Lives: Policy Demands for Black Power, Freedom & Justice*, online at https://policy.m4bl.org. Ryan's assessment was communicated by email on September 8, 2016.

92   See Alexander Sammon, "A History of Native Americans Protesting the Dakota Access Pipeline," *Mother Jones* (September 9, 2016), updated version online at http://www.motherjones.com/environment/2016/09/dakota-access-pipeline-protest-timeline sioux-standing-rock-jill-stein; Rebecca Solnit, "Standing Rock protests: this is only the beginning," *The Guardian* (September 12, 2016), online at https://www.theguardian.com/us-news/2016/sep/12/north-dakota-standing-rock-protests-civil-rights; Nadia

Prupis, "'All Out War' in North Dakota as Police Arrest 141 Water Protectors: Activists vow to keep up resistance to Dakota pipeline," *Common Dreams* (October 28, 2016), online at http://www. commondreams.org/news/2016/10/28/all-out-war-north-dakota-police-arrest-141-water-protectors.

Pacifism as Pathology: Notes on an American Pseudopraxis

by Ward Churchill

> It is the obligation of every person who claims to oppose oppression to resist the oppressor by every means at his or her disposal. Not to engage in physical resistance, armed resistance to oppression, is to serve the interests of the oppressor; no more, no less. There are no exceptions to the rule, no easy out . . .
>
> —Assata Shakur, 1984

Pacifism, the ideology of nonviolent political action, has become axiomatic and all but universal among the more progressive elements of contemporary mainstream North America. With a jargon ranging from a peculiar mishmash of borrowed or fabricated pseudospiritualism to "Gramscian" notions of prefigurative socialization, pacifism appears as the common denominator linking otherwise disparate "white dissident" groupings. Always, it promises that the harsh realities of state power can be transcended via good feelings and purity of purpose rather than by self-defense and resort to combat.

Pacifists, with seemingly endless repetition, pronounce that the negativity of the modem corporate-fascist state will atrophy through defection and neglect once there is a sufficiently positive social vision to take its place ("What if they gave a war and nobody came?"). Known in the Middle Ages as alchemy, such insistence on the repetition of insubstantial themes and failed experiments to obtain a desired result has long been consigned to the realm of fantasy, discarded by all but the most wishful or cynical (who use it to manipulate people).[1]

I don't deny the obviously admirable emotional content of the pacifist perspective. Surely we can all agree that the world should become a place of cooperation, peace, and harmony. Indeed, it *would* be nice if everything would just get better while nobody got hurt, including the oppressor who (temporarily and misguidedly) makes everything bad. Emotional niceties, however, do not render a viable politics. As with most delusions designed to avoid rather than confront unpleasant truths (Lenin's premise that the sort of state he created would wither away under "correct conditions" comes to mind),[2] the pacifist fantasy is inevitably doomed to failure by circumstance.

Even the most casual review of twentieth century history reveals the graphic contradictions of the pacifist posture, the costs of its continued practice, and its fundamental ineffectiveness in accomplishing its purported transformative mission.[3] Nonetheless, we are currently beset by "nonviolent revolutionary leaders" who habitually revise historical fact as a means of offsetting their doctrine's glaring practical deficiencies and by the spectacle of expressly pacifist organizations claiming (apparently in all seriousness) to be standing "in solidarity" with practitioners of armed resistance in Central America, Africa, and elsewhere.[4]

Despite its inability to avert a revitalized militarism in the United States, the regeneration of overt racism, and a general rise in native fascism, pacifism—the stuff of the spent mass movements of the 1960s—not only continues as the normative form of "American activism" but seems to have recently experienced a serious resurgence.[5] The purpose here is to examine the pacifist phenomenon briefly in both its political and psychological dimensions, with an eye toward identifying the relationship between a successful reactionary order, on the one hand, and a pacifist domestic opposition, on the other.

Like Lambs to the Slaughter

> I have never been able to bring myself to trust anyone who claims to have saved a Jew from the SS. The fact is that the Jews were not saved . . . no one took the steps necessary to save them, even themselves.
>
> —Simon Wiesenthal, 1967

Pacifism possesses a sublime arrogance in its implicit assumption that its adherents can somehow dictate the terms of struggle in any contest with the state.[6] Such a supposition seems unaccountable in view of the actual record of passive/nonviolent resistance to state power. Although a number of examples can be mustered with which to illustrate this point—including Buddhist resistance to U.S. policies in Indochina and the sustained efforts made to terminate white supremacist rule in southern Africa—none seems more appropriate than the Jewish experience in Hitlerian Germany (and later in the whole of occupied Europe).

The record is quite clear that, while a range of pacifist forms of countering the implications of nazism occurred within the German Jewish community during the 1930s, they offered virtually no physical opposition to the consolidation of the nazi state.[7] To the contrary, there is strong evidence that orthodox Jewish leaders counseled "social responsibility" as the best antidote to nazism, while crucial political formulations such as the zionist *Haganah* and *Mossad LeAliyah Bet* actually seem to have attempted to coopt the nazi agenda for their own purposes, entering into cooperative relations with the SS Jewish Affairs Bureau and trying to use forced immigration of Jews as a pretext for establishing a "Jewish homeland" in Palestine.[8]

All of this was apparently done in an effort to manipulate the political climate in Germany—by "not exacerbating conditions" and "not alienating the German people any further"—in a manner more favorable to Jews than the nazis were calling for.[9] In the end, of course, the nazis imposed the "final solution to the Jewish question," but by then the dynamics of passive resistance were so entrenched in the Jewish *zeitgeist* (the nazis having been in power a full decade) that a sort of passive accommodation prevailed. Jewish leaders took their people, quietly and nonviolently, first into the ghettos, and then onto trains "evacuating" them to the East. Armed resistance was still widely held to be "irresponsible."[10]

Eventually, the SS could count upon the brunt of the nazi liquidation policy being carried out by the *Sonderkommandos*, which were composed of the Jews themselves. It was largely Jews who dragged the gassed bodies of their exterminated people to the crematoria in death camps such as Auschwitz/Birkenau, each motivated by the desire to prolong his own life. Even this became rationalized as "resistance": the very act of surviving was viewed as "defeating" the nazi program.[11] By 1945, Jewish passivity and nonviolence in the face of the *Weltanschauung der Untermenschen* had done nothing to prevent the loss of millions of lives.[12]

The phenomenon sketched above must lead to the obvious question: "[How could] millions of men [*sic*] like us walk to their death without resistance?"[13] In turn, the mere asking of the obvious has spawned a veritable cottage industry among Jewish intellectuals, each explaining how it was that "the process" had left the Jewish people "no choice" but to go along, to remain passive, to proceed in accordance with their aversion to violence right up to the doors of the crematoria—and beyond.[14] From this perspective, there was nothing truly lacking in the Jewish performance; the Jews were simply and solely blameless victims of a genocidal system over which it was quite impossible for them to extend any measure of control.[15]

The Jews having suffered horribly under nazi rule,[16] it has come to be considered in exceedingly poor taste—"antisemitic," according to the logic of the Anti-Defamation League of B'nai B'rith—to suggest that there was indeed something very wrong with the nature of the Jewish response to nazism, that the mainly pacifist forms of resistance exhibited by the Jewish community played directly into the hands of their execution-ers.[17] Objectively, there *were* alternatives, and one need not look to the utterances of some "lunatic fringe" to find them articulated.

Even such a staid and conservative political commen-tator as Bruno Bettelheim, a former concentration camp inmate, has offered astute analysis of the role of passivity and nonviolence in amplifying the magnitude of the Holocaust. Regarding the single known instance in which inmates physi-cally revolted at Auschwitz, he observes that:

> In the single revolt of the twelfth Sonderkommando, seventy SS were killed, including one commissioned officer and seventeen non-commissioned offic-ers; one of the crematoria was totally destroyed and another severely damaged. True, all eight hundred and fifty-three of the kommando died. But . . . the one Sonderkommando which revolted and took such a heavy toll of the enemy did not die much differently than all the other Sonderkommandos.[18]

Aside from pointing out that the Jews had literally nothing to lose (and quite a lot to gain in terms of human dignity) by engaging in open revolt against the SS, Bettelheim goes much further, noting that such actions both in and outside the death camps stood a reasonable prospect of greatly imped-ing the extermination process.[19] He states flatly that even individualized armed resistance could have made the Final Solution a cost-prohibitive proposition for the nazis:

> There is little doubt that the [Jews], who were able to provide themselves with so much, could have pro-vided themselves with a gun or two had they wished.

> They could have shot down one or two of the SS men
> who came for them. The loss of an SS with every Jew
> arrested would have noticeably hindered the function-
> ing of the police state.[20]

Returning to the revolt of the twelfth *Sonderkommando*,
Bettelheim observes that:

> They did only what we would expect all human beings
> to do; to use their death, if they could not save their
> lives, to weaken or hinder the enemy as much as pos-
> sible; to use even their doomed selves for making
> extermination harder, or maybe impossible, not a
> smooth-running process. . . . If they could do it, so
> could others. Why didn't they? Why did they throw
> their lives away instead of making things hard for
> the enemy? Why did they make a present of their
> very being to the SS instead of to their families, their
> friends, even to their fellow prisoners?[21]
>
> Rebellion could only have saved either the life they
> were going to lose anyway, or the lives of others. . . .
> Inertia it was that led millions of Jews into the ghettos
> the SS had created for them. It was inertia that made
> hundreds of thousands of Jews sit home, waiting for
> their executioners.[22]

Bettelheim describes this inertia, which he considers the
basis for Jewish passivity in the face of genocide, as being
grounded in a profound desire for "business as usual," the
following of rules, the need to not accept reality or to act
upon it. Manifested in the irrational belief that in remaining "reasonable and responsible," unobtrusively resisting by
continuing "normal" day-to-day activities proscribed by the
nazis through the Nuremberg Laws and other infamous legislation, and "not alienating anyone," this attitude implied
that a more or less humane Jewish policy might be morally
imposed upon the nazi state by Jewish pacifism itself.[23]

Thus, Bettelheim continues:

> The persecution of the Jews was aggravated, slow step
> by slow step, when no violent fighting back occurred.
> It may have been Jewish acceptance, without retalia-
> tory fight, of ever harsher discrimination and degrada-
> tion that first gave the SS the idea that they could be
> gotten to the point where they would walk into the
> gas chambers on their own. . . . In the deepest sense,
> the walk to the gas chamber was only the last conse-
> quence of the philosophy of business as usual.[24]

Given this, Bettelheim can do little else but conclude—correctly, by any reasonable estimation—that the postwar
rationalization and apologia for the Jewish response to
nazism serves to "stress how much we all wish to subscribe to
this business as usual philosophy, and forget that it hastens
our own destruction . . . to glorify the attitude of going on
with business as usual, even in a holocaust."[25]

An Essential Contradiction

> I have no intention of being a good Jew, led into the
> ovens like some sheep.
>
> —Abbie Hoffman, 1969

The example of the Jews under nazism is, to be sure, extreme.
History affords us few comparable models by which to assess
the effectiveness of nonviolent opposition to state policies,
at least in terms of the scale and rapidity with which consequences were visited upon the passive. Yet it is precisely this
extremity, which makes the example useful; the Jewish experience reveals with stark clarity the basic illogic at the very
core of pacifist conceptions of morality and political action.[26]

Proponents of nonviolent political "praxis" are inherently placed in the position of claiming to meet the armed
might of the state via an asserted moral superiority attached
to the renunciation of arms and physical violence altogether.

It follows that the state has demonstrated, a priori, its fundamental immorality/illegitimacy by arming itself in the first place. A certain psychological correlation is typically offered wherein the "good" and "positive" social vision (Eros) held by the pacifist opposition is posed against the "bad" or "negative" realities (Thanatos) evidenced by the state. The correlation lends itself readily to "good versus evil" dichotomies, fostering a view of social conflict as a morality play.[27]

There can be no question but that there is a superficial logic to the analytical equation thus established. The Jews in their disarmed and passive resistance to German oppression during the 1930s and '40s were certainly "good"; the nazis—as well armed as any group in history up to that point—might undoubtedly be assessed as a force of unmitigated "evil."[28] Such binary correlations might also be extended to describe other sets of historical forces: Gandhi's Indian Union (good) versus troops of the British Empire (evil) and Martin Luther King Jr.'s nonviolent Civil Rights Movement (good) versus a host of Klansmen and Southern cracker police (evil) offer ready examples.

In each case, the difference between them can be (and often is) attributed to the relative willingness/unwillingness of the opposing sides to engage in violence. And, in each case, it can be (and has been) argued that good ultimately overcame the evil it confronted, achieving political gains and at least temporarily dissipating a form of social violence. To the extent that Eichmann was eventually tried in Jerusalem for his part in the genocide of the Jewish people, that India has passed from the control of England, and that Mississippi blacks can now register to vote with comparative ease, it may be (and is) contended that there is a legacy of nonviolent political success informing the praxis of contemporary pacifism.[29]

It becomes quite possible for sensitive, refined, and morally developed individuals to engage in socially transformative political action while rejecting violence as a means or method containing a positive as well as negative utility.

The teleological assumption here is that a sort of "negation of the negation" is involved, that the "power of nonviolence" can in itself be used to supplant the offending societal violence represented in the formation of state power. The key to the whole is that it *has been done*, as the survival of at least some of the Jews, the decolonization of India, and the enfranchisement of Southern American blacks demonstrate.[30]

This tidy scheme, pleasing as it may be on an emotional level, brings up more questions than it answers. An obvious question is that if nonviolence is to be taken as the emblem of Jewish goodness in the face of nazi evil, how is one to account for the revolt of the twelfth *Sonderkommando* mentioned by Bettelheim or scattered incidents of the same type which occurred at other death camps such as Sobibór and Treblinka?[31] What of the several thousand participants in the sole mass uprising of Jews outside the camps, the armed revolt of the Warsaw Ghetto during April and May 1943?[32] May it rightly be suggested that those who took up arms against their executioners crossed the same symbolic line demarcating good and evil, becoming "the same" as the SS?[33] One may assume for the moment that such a gross distortion of reality is hardly the intent of even the hardiest pacifist polemicists, although it may well be an intrinsic aspect of their position. Worse than this is the inconsistency of nonviolent premises. For instance, it has been abundantly documented that nazi policy toward the Jews, from 1941 onward, was bound up in the notion that extermination would proceed until such time as the entire Jewish population within German occupied territory was liquidated.[34] There is no indication whatsoever that nonviolent intervention/mediation from any quarter held the least prospect of halting, or even delaying, the genocidal process. To the contrary, there is evidence that efforts by neutral parties such as the Red Cross had the effect of *speeding up* the slaughter.[35]

That the Final Solution was halted at a point short of its full realization was due solely to the massive application of armed force against Germany (albeit for reasons other than the salvation of the Jews). Left to a pacifist prescription for the altering of offensive state policies, and the effecting of positive social change, "World Jewry"—at least in its Eurasian variants—would have suffered total extermination by mid-1946 at the latest. Even the highly symbolic trial of SS Obersturmbannführer (Lt. Colonel) Adolf Eichmann could not be accomplished by nonviolent means but required armed action by an Israeli paramilitary unit fifteen years after the last death camp was closed by Russian tanks.[36]

There is, moreover, every indication that adherence to pacifist principles would have resulted in Eichmann's permanent avoidance of justice, living out his life in reasonable comfort until—to paraphrase his own assessment—he leapt into the grave laughing at the thought of having killed six million Jews.[37] With reference to the Jewish experience, nonviolence was a catastrophic failure, and only the most extremely violent intervention by others saved Europe's Jews at the last moment from slipping over the brink of utter extinction. Small wonder that the survivors insist, "Never again!"[38]

While other examples are less crystalline in their implications, they are instructive. The vaunted career of Gandhi exhibits characteristics of a calculated strategy of nonviolence salvaged only by the existence of violent peripheral processes.[39] While it is true that the great Indian leader never deviated from his stance of passive resistance to British colonization, and that in the end England found it cost prohibitive to continue its effort to assert control in the face of his opposition, it is equally true that the Gandhian success must be viewed in the context of a general decline in British power brought about by two world wars within a thirty-year period.[40]

Prior to the decimation of British troop strength and the virtual bankruptcy of the Imperial treasury during World War II, Gandhi's movement showed little likelihood of forcing England's abandonment of India. Without the global violence that destroyed the Empire's ability to forcibly control its colonial territories (and passive populations), India might have continued indefinitely in the pattern of minority rule marking the majority of South Africa's modern history, the first locale in which the Gandhian recipe for liberation struck the reef of reality.[41] Hence, while the Mahatma and his followers were able to remain "pure," their victory was contingent upon others physically gutting their opponents for them.

Similarly, the limited success attained by Martin Luther King Jr. and his disciples in the United States during the 1960s, using a strategy consciously guided by Gandhian principles of nonviolence, owes a considerable debt to the existence of less pacifist circumstances. King's movement had attracted considerable celebrity but precious little in the way of tangible political gains prior to the emergence of a trend consummated in 1969 by redesignation of the Student Nonviolent Coordinating Committee (SNCC; more or less the campus arm of King's Civil Rights Movement) as the Student National Coordinating Committee.[42]

The SNCC's action (precipitated by non-pacifists such as Stokely Carmichael and H. Rap Brown) occurred in the context of armed self-defense tactics being employed by rural black leaders such as Robert F. Williams, and the eruption of black urban enclaves in Detroit, Newark, Watts, Harlem, and elsewhere. It also coincided with the increasing need of the American state for internal stability due to the unexpectedly intense and effective armed resistance mounted by the Vietnamese against U.S. aggression in Southeast Asia.[43]

Suddenly King, previously stonewalled and redbaited by the establishment, his roster of civil rights demands evaded or dismissed as being "too radical" and "premature," found himself viewed as the lesser of evils by the state.[44] He was duly anointed the "responsible black leader" in the media, and the final elements of his cherished civil rights agenda were largely incorporated into law in 1968, along with provisions designed to neutralize "Black Power Militants" such as Carmichael and Brown.[45] Without the specter, real or perceived, of a violent black revolution at large in America during a time of war, King's nonviolent strategy was basically impotent in concrete terms. As one of his Northern organizers, William Jackson, put it to me in 1969:

> There are a lot of reasons why I can't get behind fomenting violent actions like riots, and *none* of 'em are religious. It's all pragmatic politics. But I'll tell you what: I *never* let a riot slide by. I'm always the first one down at city hall and testifying before Congress, tellin' 'em, "See? If you guys'd been dealing with *us* all along, this never would have happened." It gets results, man. Like nothin' else, y'know? The thing is that Rap Brown and the Black Panthers are just about the best things that ever happened to the Civil Rights Movement.

Jackson's exceedingly honest, if more than passingly cynical, outlook was tacitly shared by King.[46] The essential contradiction inherent to pacifist praxis is that, for survival itself, any nonviolent confrontation of state power must ultimately depend either on the state refraining from unleashing some real measure of its potential violence or the active presence of some counterbalancing violence of precisely the sort pacifism professes to reject as a political option.

Absurdity clearly abounds when suggesting that the state will refrain from using all necessary physical force to protect against undesired forms of change and threats to its safety. Nonviolent tacticians imply (perhaps unwittingly) that the "immoral state" which they seek to transform will somehow exhibit exactly the same sort of *superior* morality they claim for themselves (i.e., at least a relative degree of nonviolence). The fallacy of such a proposition is best demonstrated by the nazi state's removal of its "Jewish threat."[47]

Violent intervention by others divides itself naturally into the two parts represented by Gandhi's unsolicited "windfall" of massive violence directed against his opponents and King's rather more conscious and deliberate utilization of incipient antistate violence as a means of advancing his own pacifist agenda.[48] History is replete with variations on these two sub-themes, but variations do little to alter the crux of the situation: there simply has never been a revolution, or even a substantial social reorganization, brought into being on the basis of the principles of pacifism.[49] In every instance, violence has been an integral *requirement* of the process of transforming the state.

Pacifist praxis (or, more appropriately, pseudopraxis), if followed to its logical conclusions, leaves its adherents with but two possible outcomes to their line of action:

1. To render themselves perpetually ineffectual (and conse-quently unthreatening) in the face of state power, in which case they will likely be largely ignored by the status quo and self-eliminating in terms of revolutionary potential;

2. To make themselves a clear and apparent danger to the state, in which case they are subject to physical liquida-tion by the status quo and are self-eliminating in terms of revolutionary potential.

In either event—mere ineffectuality or suicide—the objective conditions leading to the necessity for social revolu-tion remain unlikely to be altered by purely pacifist strategies. As these conditions typically include war, the induced star-vation of whole populations, and the like, pacifism and its attendant sacrifice of life cannot even be rightly said to have substantially impacted the level of evident societal violence. The mass suffering that revolution is intended to alleviate will continue as the revolution strangles itself on the altar of "nonviolence."[50]

The Comfort Zone

> Speak not of revolution until you are willing to eat
> rats to survive . . .
>
> —The Last Poets, 1970

Regardless of the shortcomings of pacifism as a methodo-logical approach to revolution, there is nothing inherent in its basic impulse that prevents real practitioners from experiencing the revolutionary ethos. Rather, as already noted, the emotional content of the principle of nonviolence is tantamount to a gut-level rejection of much, or even all, that the present social order stands for—an intrinsically revolutionary perspective. The question is not the motivations of real pacifists, but instead the nature of a strategy by which the revolution may be won, at a minimum sacrifice to all concerned.

This of course assumes that sacrifice is *being* made by all concerned. Here, it becomes relatively easy to separate the wheat from the chaff among America's proponents of "nonviolent opposition." While the premise of pacifism necessarily precludes engaging in violent acts directed at others, even for reasons of self-defense, it does not prevent its adherents from themselves incurring physical punishment in pursuit of social justice. In other words, there is nothing of a doctrinal nature barring real pacifists from running real risks.

And indeed they do. Since at least the early Christians, devout pacifists have been sacrificing themselves while standing up for what they believe in against the armed might of those they consider wrong. Gandhi's followers perished by the thousands, allowed themselves to be beaten and maimed en masse, and clogged India's penal system in their campaign to end British rule.[51] Field organizers adhering to King's version of Gandhian principles showed incredible bravery in confronting the Jim Crow sheriffs and other racist thugs of the South, and many paid with their lives on lonely back roads.[52]

Another type of pacifist action which became a symbol for the nonviolent antiwar movement was that of a Buddhist monk Thích Quảng Đức, who immolated himself on a Saigon street on June 11, 1963. Đức's protest against growing U.S. involvement in his country was quickly followed by similar actions by other Vietnamese bonzes and, on November 2, 1965, by an American Quaker, Norman Morrison, who burned himself in front of the Pentagon to protest increasing levels of U.S. troop commitment in Indochina.[53] Whatever the strategic value one may place upon the actions of Morrison and the Buddhists—and it must be acknowledged that the U.S. grip on Vietnam rapidly tightened after the self-immolations began,[54] while America's troop strength in Southeast Asia spiraled from some 125,000 at the time of Morrison's suicide to more than 525,000 barely two years later—they were unquestionably courageous people, entirely willing to face the absolute certainty of the most excruciating death in pursuit of their professed ideals. Although the effectiveness of their tactics is open to question, their courage and integrity certainly are not.

In a less severe fashion, there are many other examples of American pacifists putting themselves on the line for their beliefs. The Berrigan brothers, Philip and Daniel, clearly qualify in this regard, as do a number of others who took direct action against the Selective Service System and certain U.S. military targets during the late 1960s and early 1970s.[55] Cadres of Witness for Peace placed their bodies between CIA-sponsored contra guerrillas and their intended civilian victims along the Nicaragua/Honduras border during the 1980s.[56] Members of both Greenpeace and Earth First! have been known to take considerable chances with their own well-being in their advocacy of a range of environmental issues.[57]

The list of principled and self-sacrificing pacifists and pacifist acts could undoubtedly be extended and, ineffectual or not, these people are admirable in their own right. Unfortunately, they represent the exception rather than the rule of pacifist performance in the United States. For every example of serious and committed pacifist activism emerging from the normative mass of American nonviolent movements since 1965, one could cite scores of countering instances in which only lip service was paid to the ideals of action and self-sacrifice.

The question central to the emergence and maintenance of nonviolence as the oppositional foundation of American activism has not been the truly pacifist formulation, "How can we forge a revolutionary politics within which we can avoid inflicting violence on others?" On the contrary, a more accurate guiding question has been, "What sort of politics might I engage in which will both allow me to posture as a progressive *and* allow me to avoid incurring harm to *myself?*" Hence, the trappings of pacifism have been subverted to establish a sort of "politics of the comfort zone," not only akin to what Bettelheim termed "the philosophy of business as usual" and devoid of perceived risk to its advocates but minus any conceivable revolutionary impetus as well.[58] The intended revolutionary content of true pacifist activism—the sort practiced by the Gandhian movement, the Berrigans, and Norman Morrison—is thus isolated and subsumed in the United States, even among the ranks of self-professing participants.

Such a situation must abort whatever limited utility pacifist tactics might have, absent other and concurrent forms of struggle, as a socially transformative method. Yet the history of the American left over the past decade shows too clearly that the more diluted the substance embodied in "pacifist practice," the louder the insistence of its subscribers that nonviolence is the *only* mode of action "appropriate and acceptable within the context of North America," and the greater the effort to ostracize, or even stifle, divergent types of actions.[59] Such strategic hegemony exerted by proponents of this truncated range of tactical options has done much to foreclose on whatever revolutionary potential may be said to exist in modern America.

Is such an assessment too harsh? One need only attend a mass demonstration (ostensibly directed against the policies of the state) in any U.S. city to discover the answer. One will find hundreds, sometimes thousands, assembled in orderly fashion, listening to selected speakers calling for an end to this or that aspect of lethal state activity, carrying signs "demanding" the same thing, welcoming singers who enunciate lyrically on the worthiness of the demonstrators' agenda, as well as the plight of the various victims they are there to "defend," and—typically—the whole thing is quietly disbanded with exhortations to the assembled to "keep working" on the matter and to please sign a petition or write letters to legislators requesting that they alter or abandon offending undertakings.

Throughout the whole charade it will be noticed that the state is represented by a uniformed police presence keeping a discreet distance and not interfering with the activities. And why should they? The organizers of the demonstration will have gone through "proper channels" to obtain permits *required by the state* and instructions as to where they will be allowed to assemble, how long they will be allowed to stay and, should a march be involved in the demonstration, along which routes they will be allowed to walk.

Surrounding the larger mass of demonstrators can be seen others—an elite. Adorned with green (or white or powder blue) armbands, their function is to ensure that demonstrators remain "responsible," not deviating from the state-sanctioned plan of protest. Individuals or small groups who attempt to spin off from the main body, entering areas to which the state has denied access (or some other unapproved activity) are headed off by these armbanded "marshals" who argue—pointing to the nearby police—that "troublemaking" will only "exacerbate an already tense situation" and "provoke violence," thereby "alienating those we are attempting to reach."[60] In some ways, the voice of the "good Jews" can be heard to echo plainly over the years.

At this juncture, the confluence of interests between the state and the mass nonviolent movement could not be clearer. The role of the police, whose function is to enforce state policy by minimizing disruption of its procedures, should be in natural conflict with that of a movement purporting to challenge these same policies and, indeed, to seek transformation of the state itself.[61] However, with apparent perverseness, the police find themselves serving as mere backups (or props) to self-policing (now euphemistically termed "peacekeeping" rather than the more accurate "marshaling") efforts of the alleged opposition's own membership. Both sides of the "contestation" concur that the smooth functioning of state processes must not be physically disturbed, at least not in any significant way.[62]

All of this is within the letter and spirit of cooptive forms of sophisticated self-preservation appearing as an integral aspect of the later phases of bourgeois democracy.[63] It dovetails well with more shopworn methods such as the electoral process and has been used by the state as an innovative means of conducting public opinion polls, which better hide rather than eliminate controversial policies.[64] Even the movement's own sloganeering tends to bear this out from time to time, as when Students for a Democratic Society (SDS) coined the catchphrase of its alternative to the polling place: "Vote with your feet, vote in the street."[65]

Of course, any movement seeking to project a credible self-image as something other than just one more variation of accommodation to state power must ultimately establish its "militant" oppositional credentials through the media in a manner more compelling than rhetorical speechifying and the holding of impolite placards ("Fuck the War" was always a good one) at rallies.[66] Here, the time-honored pacifist notion of "civil disobedience" is given a new twist by the adherents of nonviolence in America. Rather than pursuing Gandhi's (or, to a much lesser extent, King's) method of using passive bodies to literally clog the functioning of the state apparatus—regardless of the cost to those doing the clogging—the American nonviolent movement has increasingly opted for "symbolic actions."[67]

The centerpiece of such activity usually involves an arrest, either of a token figurehead of the movement (or a small, selected group of them) or a mass arrest of some sort. In the latter event, "arrest training" is generally provided—and lately has become "required" by movement organizers—by the same marshals who will later ensure that crowd control police units will be left with little or nothing to do. This is to ensure that "no one gets hurt" in the process of being arrested and that the police are not inconvenienced by disorganized arrest procedures.[68]

The event which activates the arrests is typically preplanned, well-publicized in advance, and, more often than not, literally coordinated with the police—often including estimates by organizers concerning how many arrestees will likely be involved. Generally speaking, such "extreme statements" will be scheduled to coincide with larger-scale peaceful demonstrations so that a considerable audience of "committed" bystanders (and, hopefully, NBC/CBS/ABC/CNN) will be on hand to applaud the bravery and sacrifice of those arrested; most of the bystanders will, of course, have considered reasons why they themselves are unprepared to "go so far" as to be arrested.[69] The specific sort of action designed to precipitate the arrests themselves usually involves one of the following: (a) sitting down in a restricted area and refusing to leave when ordered; (b) stepping across an imaginary line drawn on the ground by a police representative; (c) refusing to disperse at the appointed time; (d) chaining or padlocking the doors to a public building. When things *really* get heavy, those seeking to be arrested may pour blood (real or ersatz) on something of "symbolic value."[70]

As a rule, those arrested are cooperative in the extreme, meekly allowing police to lead them to waiting vans or buses for transportation to whatever station house or temporary facility has been designated as the processing point. In especially "militant" actions, arrestees go limp, undoubtedly severely taxing the state's repressive resources by forcing the police to carry them bodily to the vans or buses (monitored all the while by volunteer attorneys, who are there to ensure that such "police brutality" as pushing, shoving, or dropping an arrestee does not occur). In either event, the arrestees sit quietly in their assigned vehicles—or sing "We Shall Overcome" and other favorites—as they are driven away for booking. The typical charges levied will be trespassing, creating a public disturbance, or being a public nuisance. In the heavy instances, the charge may be escalated to malicious mischief or even destruction of public property. Either way, other than in exceptional circumstances, everyone will be assigned an arraignment date and released on personal recognizance or a small cash bond, home in time for dinner (and to review their exploits on the six o'clock news).[71]

In the unlikely event that charges are not dismissed prior to arraignment (the state having responded to symbolic actions by engaging largely in symbolic selective prosecutions), the arrestee will appear on the appointed date in a room resembling a traffic court where s/he will be allowed to plead guilty, pay a minimal fine, and go home. Repeat offenders may be "sentenced" to pay a somewhat larger fine (which, of course, goes into state accounts underwriting the very policies the arrestees ostensibly oppose) or even to perform a specific number of "public service hours" (promoting police/ community relations, for example).[72] It is almost unheard of for arrestees to be sentenced to jail time for the simple reason that most jails are already overflowing with less "principled" individuals, most of them rather unpacifist in nature, and many of whom have caused the state a considerably greater degree of displeasure than the nonviolent movement, which claims to seek its radical alteration.[73]

For those arrestees who opt to plead not guilty to the charges they themselves literally arranged to incur, a trial date will be set. They will thereby accrue another symbolic advantage by exercising their right to explain why they did whatever they did before a judge and jury. They may then loftily contend that it is the state, rather than themselves, that is really criminal. Their rights satisfied, they will then generally be sentenced to exactly the same penalty which would have been levied had they pleaded guilty at their arraignment (plus court costs) and go home. A few will be sentenced to a day or two in jail as an incentive not to waste court time with such pettiness in the future. A few less will refuse to pay whatever fine is imposed and receive as much as thirty days in jail (usually on work release) as an alternative; a number of these have opted to pen "prison letters" during the period of their brief confinement, underscoring the sense of symbolic (rather than literal) self-sacrifice which is sought.[74]

The trivial nature of this level of activity does not come fully into focus until it is juxtaposed to the sorts of state activity that the nonviolent movement claims to be "working on." A brief sampling of prominent issues addressed by the American opposition since 1965 will suffice for purposes of illustration: the U.S. escalation of the ground war in Southeast Asia to a level where more than a million lives were lost, the saturation bombing of Vietnam (another one to two million killed), the expansion of the Vietnam war into all of Indochina (costing perhaps another two to three million lives when the intentional destruction of Cambodia's farmland and resultant mass starvation are considered), U.S. sponsorship of the Pinochet coup in Chile (at least another 10,000 dead), U.S. underwriting of the Salvadoran oligarchy (50,000 lives at a minimum), U.S. support of the Guatemalan junta (perhaps 200,000 killed since 1954), and efforts to destabilize the Sandinista government in Nicaragua (at least 20,000 dead).[75] A far broader sample of comparably lethal activities has gone unopposed altogether.[76]

While the human costs of continuing American business as usual have registered well into the seven-digit range (and possibly higher), the nonviolent "opposition" in the United States has not only restricted its tactics almost exclusively to the symbolic arena denoted above but has actively endeavored to prevent others from going further. The methods employed to this end have generally been restricted to the deliberate stigmatizing, isolation, and minimization of other potentials—as a means of neutralizing, or at least containing them—although at times it seems to have crossed over into collaboration with state efforts to bring about their outright liquidation.[77]

The usual approach has been a consistent a priori dismissal of any one person or group attempting to move beyond the level of symbolic action as "abandoning the original spirit [of North American oppositional politics] and taking the counterproductive path of small-scale violence now and organizing for serious armed struggle later."[78] This is persistently coupled with attempts to diminish the importance of actions aimed at concrete rather than symbolic effects, epitomized in the question framed by Sam Brown, a primary organizer of the November 1969 Moratorium to End the War in Vietnam (when perhaps 5,000 broke free of a carefully orchestrated schedule of passive activities): "What's more important, that a bunch of scruffy people charged the Justice Department, or that [several hundred thousand people] were in the same place at one time to sing?"[79]

Not only was such "violence" as destroying property and scuffling with police proscribed in the view of Moratorium organizers but also any tendency to utilize the incredible mass of assembled humanity in any way which might tangibly interfere with the smooth physical functioning of the governing apparatus in the nation's capital (e.g., nonviolent civil disobedience on the order of, say, systematic traffic blockages and huge sit-ins).[80]

Unsurprisingly, this same mentality manifested itself even more clearly a year and a half later with the open boycott by pacifism's "responsible leadership" (and most of their committed followers) of the National Peace Action Coalition's planned "May Day Demonstration" in Washington. Although in some ways the war had escalated (e.g., increasingly heavy bombing) since the largest symbolic protest in American history—the Moratorium fielded approximately one million passive demonstrators nationwide—it was still held that May Day organizer Rennie Davis's intent to "show the government that it will no longer be able to control its own society unless it ends the war NOW!" was "going too far."[81] It was opined that although Davis's plan to mount a "spring offensive" in the capitol did not call for violent acts, its disruption of business as usual was likely to "provoke a violent response from officials."[82]

Even more predictably, advocates of nonviolence felt compelled to counter such emergent trends as the SDS Revolutionary Youth Movement, Youth Against War and Fascism, and Weatherman.[83] Calling for nonattendance at the demonstrations of "irresponsible" organizations attempting to build a "fighting movement among white radicals," and wittily coining derogatory phrases to describe them, the oppositional mainstream did its utmost to thwart possible positive developments coming from such unpacifist quarters. In the end, the stigmatized organizations themselves institutionalized this imposed isolation, their frustration with attempting to break the inertia of symbolic opposition to the status quo converted into a "politics of despair" relying solely on violent actions undertaken by a network of tiny underground cells.[84]

The *real* anathema to the nonviolent mass, however, turned out not to be white splinter groups such as Weatherman. Rather, it came from a militant black nationalism embodied in the Black Panther Party for Self-Defense. After nearly a decade of proclaiming its "absolute solidarity" with the liberatory efforts of American blacks, pacifism found itself confronted during the late 1960s with the appearance of a cohesive organization that consciously linked the oppression of the black community to the exploitation of people the world over and *programmatically* asserted the same right to armed self-defense acknowledged as the due of liberation movements abroad.[85]

As the Panthers evidenced signs of making significant headway, organizing first in their home community of Oakland and then nationally, the state perceived something more threatening than yet another series of candlelight vigils. It reacted accordingly, targeting the Panthers for physical elimination. When Party cadres responded (as promised) by meeting the violence of repression with armed resistance, the bulk of their "principled" white support evaporated. This horrifying retreat rapidly isolated the Party from any possible mediating or buffering from the full force of state terror and left its members nakedly exposed to "surgical termination" by special police units.[86]

To cover this default on true pacifist principles—which call upon adherents not to run for safety but, in the manner of Witness for Peace, to interpose their bodies as a means of alleviating violence—it became fashionable to observe that the Panthers were "as bad as the cops" in that they had resorted to arms (a view which should give pause when one recalls the twelfth *Sonderkommando*); they had "brought this on themselves" when they "provoked violence" by refusing the state an uncontested right to maintain the lethal business as usual it had visited upon black America since the inception of the Republic.[87]

In deciphering the meaning of this pattern of response to groups such as the Panthers, Weatherman, and others who have attempted to go beyond a more symbolic protest of, say, genocide, it is important to look behind the clichés customarily used to explain the American pacifist posture (however revealing these may be in themselves). More to the point than concerns that the groups such as the Panthers "bring this [violent repression] on themselves" is the sentiment voiced by Irv Kurki, a prominent Illinois antidraft organizer, during the winter of 1969–1970:

> This idea of armed struggle or armed self-defense or whatever you want to call it . . . practiced by the Black Panther Party, the Weathermen and a few other groups is a very bad scene, a really dangerous thing for all of us. This isn't Algeria or Vietnam, it's the United

States. . . . These tactics are not only counterproductive in that they alienate people who are otherwise
very sympathetic to us . . . and lead to the sort of thing
which just happened in Chicago . . . but *they run the very
real risk of bringing the same sort of violent repression down on
all of us.* (emphasis added)[88]

Precisely. The preoccupation with avoiding actions that
might "provoke violence" is thus not based on a sincere belief
that violence will, or even can, truly be avoided. Pacifists,
no less than their nonpacifist counterparts, are quite aware
that violence *already* exists as an integral component in the
execution of state policies and requires no provocation; this
is a formative basis of their doctrine. What is at issue then
cannot be a valid attempt to stave off or even minimize violence per se. Instead, it can only be a conscious effort not
to refocus state violence in such a way that it would directly
impact American pacifists *themselves*. This is true even when
it can be shown that the tactics which could trigger such a
refocusing might in themselves alleviate a real measure of
the much more massive state-inflicted violence occurring
elsewhere; better that another 100,000 Indochinese peasants perish under a hail of cluster bombs and napalm than
America's principled progressives suffer real physical pain
while rendering their government's actions impracticable.[89]

Such conscientious avoidance of personal sacrifice (i.e.,
dodging the experience of being on the receiving end of violence not the inflicting of it) has nothing to do with the lofty
ideals and integrity by which American pacifists claim to
inform their practice. But it does explain the real nature of
such curious phenomena as movement marshals, steadfast
refusals to attempt to bring the seat of government to a stand-
still, even when a million people are on hand to accomplish
the task, and the consistently convoluted victim blaming
engaged in with regard to domestic groups such as the Black
Panther Party.[90] Massive and unremitting violence in the

colonies is appalling to right-thinking people but ultimately acceptable when compared with the unthinkable alternative that any degree of real violence might be redirected against "mother country radicals."[91]

Viewed in this light, a great many things make sense. For instance, the persistent use of the term "responsible leadership" in describing the normative nonviolent sector of North American dissent—always somewhat mysterious when applied to supposed radicals (or German Jews)—is clarified as signifying nothing substantially different from the accommodation of the status quo it implies in more conventional settings.[92] The "rules of the game" have long been established and tacitly agreed to by both sides of the ostensible "oppositional equation": demonstrations of "resistance" to state policies will be allowed so long as they do nothing to materially interfere with the implementation of those policies.[93]

The responsibility of the oppositional leadership in such a trade-off is to ensure that state processes are not threatened by substantial physical disruption; the reciprocal responsibility of the government is to guarantee the general safety of those who play according to the rules.[94] This comfortable scenario is enhanced by the mutual understanding that certain levels of "appropriate" (symbolic) protest of given policies will result in the "oppositional victory" of their modification (i.e., really a "tuning" of policy by which it may be rendered more functional and efficient, never an abandonment of fundamental policy thrusts), while efforts to move beyond this metaphorical medium of dissent will be squelched "by any means necessary" and by all parties concerned.[95] Meanwhile, the entire unspoken arrangement is larded with a layer of stridently abusive rhetoric directed by each side against the other.

We are left with a husk of opposition, a ritual form capable of affording a maudlin "I'm OK, you're OK" satisfaction to its subscribers at a psychic level but utterly useless in terms of transforming the power relations perpetuating systemic global violence.[96] Such a defect can, however, be readily sublimated within the aggregate comfort zone produced by the continuation of North American business as usual; those who remain within the parameters of nondisruptive dissent allowed by the state, their symbolic duty to the victims of U.S. policy done (and with the bases of state power wholly unchallenged), can devote themselves to the prefiguration of the revolutionary future society with which they proclaim they will replace the present social order (having, no doubt, persuaded the state to overthrow itself through the moral force of their arguments).[97] Here, concrete activities such as sexual experimentation, refinement of musical/artistic tastes, development of various meat-free diets, getting in touch with one's "id" through meditation and ingestion of hallucinogens, alteration of sex-based distribution of household chores, and waging campaigns against such "bourgeois vices" as smoking tobacco become the signifiers of "correct politics" or even "revolutionary practice." This is *as opposed to* the active and effective confrontation of state power.[98]

Small wonder that North America's ghetto, barrio, and reservation populations, along with the bulk of the white working class—people who are by and large structurally denied access to the comfort zone (both in material terms and in a corresponding inability to avoid the imposition of a relatively high degree of systemic violence)—tend either to stand aside in bemused incomprehension of such politics or to react with outright hostility. Their apprehension of the need for revolutionary change and their conception of revolutionary dynamics are necessarily at radical odds with this notion of "struggle."[99] The American nonviolent movement, which has labored so long and so hard to isolate all divergent oppositional tendencies, is in the end isolating itself, becoming ever more demographically white, middle-class, and "respectable." Eventually, unless there is a marked change in its obstinate insistence that it holds a "moral right" to absolute tactical monopoly, American pacifism will be left to "feel good about itself" while the revolution goes on without it.[100]

Let's Pretend

> Are you listening, Nixon? Johnson refused to hear us,
> and you know what happened to that ol' boy . . .
> —Benjamin Spock, November 1969

American pacifism seeks to project itself as a revolutionary alternative to the status quo.[101] Of course, such a movement or perspective can hardly acknowledge that its track record in forcing substantive change upon the state has been an approximate zero. A chronicle of significant success must be offered, even where none exists. Equally, should such a movement or perspective seek hegemony of its particular vision—again, as American pacifism has been shown to do since 1965—a certain mythological complex is required to support its contentions. Generally speaking, both needs can be accommodated within a single unified propaganda structure.[102]

For proponents of the hegemony of nonviolent political action within the American opposition, time-honored fables such as the success of Gandhi's methods (in and of themselves), and even the legacy of Martin Luther King Jr. no longer retain the freshness and vitality required to achieve the necessary result. As this has become increasingly apparent, and as the potential to bring a number of emergently dissident elements (e.g., "freezers," antinukers, environmentalists, opponents to saber-rattling in Central America and the Mideast, and so on) into some sort of centralized mass movement became greater in the mid-1980s, a freshly packaged pacifist "history" of its role in opposing the Vietnam war began to be peddled with escalating frequency and insistence.[103] It is instructive to examine several salient claims still extended by pacifist organizers.

The nonviolent mass movement against the war forced Lyndon Johnson from office when he failed to withdraw

from Vietnam (picking up a theme topical to the antiwar movement itself). Actually, as has been conclusively demonstrated, it was "Hawks" rather than "Doves" who toppled Johnson.[104] This was due to the perceived ineffectiveness with which he prosecuted the war, brought about not by pacifist parades in American streets but by the effectiveness of *Vietnamese armed resistance* to U.S. military aggression. The catalyst was the Vietnamese Tet Offensive in January 1968, after U.S. Commanding General William Westmoreland announced he had "broken their ability to fight," and the general's resultant request for another 206,000 troops to augment the more than one-half million already at his disposal.[105] At this point, the *right wing* decided that the war was lost and to begin a process of cutting losses, thereby forcing Johnson out.

To discern where the balance of power lay and begin to unravel who did what to whom, one need only consider that the antiwar candidate of the 1968 campaign (Eugene McCarthy) was never in serious contention as Johnson's replacement, and that it was the choice of the right (Richard Nixon) who became the successor.[106]

The self-sacrifice of such nonviolent oppositional tactics as draft resistance seriously impaired the functioning of the U.S. military machine (picking up another topical theme). Actually, there was not much self-sacrifice or risk involved. Of the estimated one million American males who committed draft offenses during the Vietnam era, only 25,000 (2.5 percent) were indicted, and a total of 3,250 (0.3 percent) went to prison. As many as 80,000 went into voluntary exile in Canada, where some noted the penalty of "being lonely."[107] The other 91.5 percent of these self-sacrificing individuals apparently paid no price at all, remaining in the comfort zone relative to both the military and the supposed consequences of evading it.

It may be that draft resistance on this scale somehow affected the *reserve* manpower of the military but not its main force units. What *did* affect the functioning of the military was the rapid disintegration of morale among U.S. combat troops after 1968 as a result of the effectiveness of Vietnamese *armed* resistance. The degeneration of effectiveness within the U.S. military, which eventually neutralized it in the field, included mass refusal to fight (approved, undoubtedly, by pacifists), spiraling substance abuse (ditto), and, most effectively, the assassination of commissioned and noncommissioned officers (well, that's going too far).[108]

The most effective tactic the nonviolent movement could have engaged in to impair the U.S. military was therefore the one thing it was most unprepared to consider: making the individual personal sacrifice of going *into* the military in a massive way in order to quickly subvert it.

The nonviolent mass antiwar movement's solidarity with the Vietnamese undercut the political ability of the U.S. government to continue and forced the war to an early close (a stated objective of the movement of the late 1960s). This claim is obviously closely akin to the contention concerning Johnson, although it should be recalled that even U.S. ground forces remained in Vietnam for another four years after that "victory." Actually, there was no mass antiwar movement in the United States, nonviolent or otherwise, by the time the war ended in 1975. It had begun to dissipate rapidly during the summer of 1970 in the wake of sustaining its first and only real casualties—a total of four dead at Kent State University in Ohio that spring.[109] By the time the last U.S. ground troops were withdrawn in March 1973, "Nixinger" had suspended the draft, and with the element of their personal jeopardy thus eliminated, the "principled" opposition fueling the mass movement evaporated altogether while the war did not.[110]

That the war continued for another two years with U.S. technological and economic support at the cost of hundreds of thousands of Vietnamese lives but absent even a symbolic mass American opposition worthy of the name says volumes about the nature of the nonviolent movement's "solidarity with the Vietnamese."[111] And, as always, it was the armed struggle waged by the Vietnamese themselves—without the pretense of systematic support from the American pacifists—which finally forced the war to a close.[112]

It is evident even from this brief exposition of fact versus fantasy—and the analysis could be extended to much greater length with the same results—that a certain consistency is involved. As with earlier developed mythologies concerning Gandhi and King (i.e., that their accomplishments were achieved through application of nonviolent principles alone), the current pacifist propaganda line concerning the Vietnam war reveals a truly remarkable propensity to lay claim to progress attained only through the most bitter forms of armed struggle undertaken by others (all the while blandly insisting that the "resort to violence" was/is "inappropriate" in the context of North America).[113]

This already-noted cynical mindwarp holds little appeal to those residing outside the socioeconomic limits of the American comfort zone and can hardly be expected to recruit them into adhering to nonviolence. However, this in *itself* explains much about American pacifism's real (perhaps subconscious) agenda and reconciles a range of apparent contradictions in the postures of American pacifist strategists.

The Buck Is Passed

> We support the just struggles of the NLF in Vietnam.
> —David Dellinger, 1969

It is immediately perplexing to confront the fact that many of North America's most outspoken advocates of absolute domestic nonviolence when challenging state power have consistently aligned themselves with the most powerful expressions of armed resistance to the exercise of U.S. power *abroad*. Any roster of pacifist luminaries fitting this description would include not only David Dellinger, but Joan Baez, Benjamin Spock, A.J. Muste, Holly Near, Staughton Lynd, and Noam Chomsky as well.

The situation is all the more problematic when one considers that these leaders, each in his/her own way, also advocate their followers' perpetual diversion into activities prefiguring the nature of a revolutionary society, the basis for which cannot be reasonably expected to appear through nonviolent tactics alone.[114] This apparent paradox erodes a line of reasoning that, although it has probably never been precisely formulated within the North American nonviolent movement, seems likely to have informed the thinking of its more astute leadership. Its logical contours can be sketched as follows. Since at least as early as 1916, the importance of colonial and later neocolonial exploitation of the nonindustrialized world in maintaining modern capitalist states has been increasingly well understood by the revolutionary opposition within those states.[115] Today, it is widely held that removal of neocolonial sources of material and superprofits would irrevocably undercut the viability of late capitalist states.[116]

Beginning in the late 1940s with the emergence of both decolonization mandates in international law[117] and the proliferation of armed liberation movements throughout what became known as the "Third World," it became obvious to the opposition within developed states—of which the U.S. had by then assumed hegemonic status—that precisely such an undercutting removal of profits and raw materials was occurring.[118]

It required/requires no particularly sophisticated analysis to perceive that the imposition of colonial/neocolonial forms of exploitation upon Third World populations entailed/entails a degree of systemic violence sufficient to ensure the permanence of their revolt until it succeeds.[119] Similarly, it was/is understandable that Third World revolution would continue of its own volition *whether or not* it was accompanied by overt revolutionary activity within the "mother countries" (advanced capitalist states).[120]

These understandings are readily coupled with the knowledge that the types of warfare evidenced in decolonization struggles were unlikely, under normal circumstances, to trigger superpower confrontations of the type which would threaten mother country populations (including their internal oppositions).[121] Instead, the existence of armed Third World liberation movements would necessitate a continuing range of (token) concessions by the advanced industrial states to their own populations as a means of securing the internal security required for the permanent prosecution of "brush fire wars."[122]

It follows that it is possible for the resident opposition to the advanced industrial states to rely upon the armed efforts of those in the colonies to diminish the relative power of the "mutual enemy," all the while awaiting the "right moment" to take up arms themselves, "completing the world revolution" by bringing down the state. The question then becomes one of when to "seize the time," and who—precisely—it is who will be responsible for "picking up the gun" within the mother country itself.[123]

From here it is possible to extrapolate that when state power has been sufficiently weakened by the liberation struggles of those in the colonies (read: nonwhites), the most oppressed sectors of the mother country population itself (again read nonwhites, often and accurately described as constituting internal colonies)—which are guided by motivations similar to those in the Third World—will be in a position to wage successful armed struggles from within.[124] Such dissolution of the state will mark the ushering in of the postrevolutionary era.

It is possible then to visualize a world revolutionary process in which the necessity of armed participation (and attendant physical suffering) by white radicals is marginalized or dispensed with altogether. Their role in this scenario becomes that of utilizing their already attained economic and social advantages to prefigure, both intellectually and more literally, the shape of the good life to be shared by all in the postrevolutionary context; it is presumed that they will become a (perhaps the) crucial social element, having used the "space" (comfort zone) achieved through state concessions generated by the armed pressure exerted by others to the "constructive rather than destructive purpose" of developing a "superior" model of societal relations.[125]

The function of "responsible" oppositional leadership in the mother country—as opposed to the "irresponsible" variety that might precipitate some measure of armed resistance from within before the Third World has bled itself in diminishing state power from without (and who might even go so far as to suggest whites could directly participate)—is first and foremost to link the mother country movement's inaction *symbolically and rhetorically* to Third World liberation struggles. The blatant accommodation to state power involved in this is rationalized (both to the Third Worlders *and* to the movement rank-and-file) by professions of personal and principled pacifism, as well as in the need for "working models" of nonviolent behavior in postrevolutionary society.[126]

From there, the nonviolent American movement (by now overwhelmingly composed of white "progressives") can be steered into exactly the same symbolic and rhetorical "solidarity" with an emerging nonwhite armed revolution within the United States and—voila!—positive social transformation has not only been painlessly achieved (for whites), but they (being the prefigurative nonviolent "experts" on building postrevolutionary society) have maneuvered themselves into leading roles in the aftermath.[127]

All of this, of course, is predicated on the assumption that the colonized, both within and without, will ultimately prove equal to their part, and that revolutionary transformation will actually occur. In the event that the colonizing state ultimately proves the stronger of parties in such a contest, the nonviolent movement—having restricted its concrete activities to limits sanctioned by that same state—will have a natural fallback position, being as it were only a variant

of "the loyal opposition."[128] The result of the carefully constructed balance (between professed solidarity with armed
Third World insurgents, on the one hand, and tacit accommodation to the very state power against which they fight, on
the other) is that North American adherents to nonviolence
are intended to win regardless of the outcome; the comfort
zone of "white skin privilege" is to be continued in either
event.[129]

Or this is the outcome that fence-sitting is expected to
accomplish. The range of tremendous ethical, moral, and
political problems inherent in this attitude is mostly so self-
evident as to require no further explanation or consideration
here. Before turning to the purely pathological characteristics associated with such monumental (attempted) buck-
passing, there is one other primarily political potentiality that
bears at least passing discussion. It is a possibility typically
omitted or ignored within discussions of "the praxis of nonviolence" in the United States, largely because its very existence would tend to render pacifism's pleasant (to its benefi-
ciaries) prospectus rather less rosy (read: less appealing to its
intended mass of subscribers). Undoubtedly, the oversight
is also bound up in pacifism's earlier mentioned arrogance
in presuming it holds some power of superior morality to
determine that the nonviolence of its relations to the state
will necessarily be reciprocated (even to a relative degree) in
the state's relations with pacifists.[130] Whatever the basis for
generalized silence in this regard, due consideration must be
given to the likelihood that the state, at some point along its
anticipated trajectory of strategic losses in the hinterlands,
will experience the need to reconstitute its credibility internally, to bring about the psychic consolidation of its faithful
("morale building" on the grand scale) by means of a "cleans-
ing of national life" from within.

Such a transition from liberalistic and cooptive policies to much more overtly reactionary forms is certainly not
without precedent when states perceive their international

power positions eroding, or simply undergoing substantial external threat.[131] Invariably, such circumstances entail the identification (i.e., manufacture), targeting, and elimination of some internal entity as the "subversive" element undercutting the "national will" and purpose. At such times, the state needs no, indeed can tolerate no hint of, domestic opposition; those who are "tainted" by a history of even the milder forms of "antisocial" behavior can be assured of being selected as the scapegoats required for this fascist sort of consensus building.[132]

While the precise form which might be assumed by the scapegoating involved in a consolidation of North American fascism remains unknown, it is clear that the posture of the mass nonviolent movement closely approximates that of the Jews in Germany during the 1930s. The notion that "it can't happen here" is merely a parallel to the Jewish perception that it wouldn't happen *there*; insistence on inhabiting a comfort zone even while thousands upon thousands of Third World peasants are cremated beneath canisters of American napalm is only a manifestation of "the attitude of going on with business as usual, even in a holocaust."[133] Ultimately, as Bettelheim observed, it is the dynamic of attempting to restrict opposition to state terror to symbolic and nonviolent responses which gives the state "the idea that [its victims can] be gotten to the point where they [will] walk into the gas chambers on their own."[134] And, as the Jewish experience has shown for anyone who cares to look the matter in the face, the very inertia of pacifist principles prevents any effective conversion to armed self-defense once adherents are targeted for systematic elimination by the state.

Profile of a Pathology

> I just came home from Vietnam where I spent twelve months of my life trying to pacify the population. We couldn't do it; their resistance was amazing. And

it was wrong; the process made me sick. So I came
home to join the resistance in my own country, and
I find you guys have pacified yourselves. That too
amazes me; that too makes me sick.

—Vietnam Veteran Against the War, 1970

A number of logical contradictions and fundamental misun-
derstandings of political reality present themselves within
the doctrinal corpus of American pacifist premises and
practices (both as concerns real pacifism and relative to the
modern American "comfort zone" variety). Matters of this
sort are usually remediable, at least to a significant extent,
through processes of philosophical/political dialogue, factual
correction, and the like.[135] Subscribers to the notion of pacifism, however, have proven themselves so resistant as to be
immune to conventional critique and suasion, hunkering
down instead behind a wall of "principles," *especially* when
these can be demonstrated to be lacking both logically and
practically in terms of validity, viability, and utility.[136]

The "blind faith" obstinacy inherent in this position is
thus not immediately open to pragmatic, or even empirical,
consideration. It might be more properly categorized within
the sphere of theological inquiry (particularly as regards the
fundamentalist and occult religious doctrines)—and, indeed,
many variants of pacifist dogma acknowledge strong links to
an array of sects and denominations—were it not that pacifism asserts itself (generically) not only as a functional aspect
of "the real world," but as a praxis capable of engendering revolutionary social transformation.[137] Its basic irrationalities
must therefore be taken, on their face, as seriously intended
to supplant reality itself.

Codification of essentially religious symbology and
mythology as the basis for political ideology is not lacking
in precedent and has been effectively analyzed elsewhere.[138]
Although a number of interesting aspects present themselves
in the study of any specific fusion of spiritualist impetus with

political articulation/practice, the common factor from one example to the next is a central belief that objective conditions (i.e., reality) can be altered by an act of "will" (individual or collective).[139] This is often accompanied by extremely antisocial characteristics, manifested either consciously or subconsciously.[140] The political expression of pacifism confronts us with what may be analogously described as a (mass) pathology.

As with any pathology, pacifism may be said to exhibit a characteristic symptomology by which it can be diagnosed. Salient examples of the complex of factors making up the pathology may be described as follows:

Pacifism is delusional. This symptom is marked by a range of indicators, for example, insistence that reform or adjustment of given state policies constitutes a "revolutionary agenda," insistence that holding candlelight vigils and walking down the street constitute "acts of solidarity" with those engaged in armed struggle, or—despite facts to the contrary—that such things as "the nonviolent decolonization of India" or "the antiwar movement's forcing the Vietnam war to end" actually occurred.

At another level—and again despite clear facts to the contrary—insisting that certain tactics avoid "provoking violence" (when it is already massive) or that by remaining nonviolent pacifists can "morally compel" the state to respond in kind must be considered as deep-seated and persistent delusions.[141]

Finally, it must be pointed out that many supposed "deeply principled" adherents are systematically deluding themselves that they are really pacifists at all. This facet of the symptoms is marked by a consistent avoidance of personal physical risk, an overweening attitude of personal superiority vis-à-vis those who "fail" to make overt professions of nonviolence, and sporadic lapses into rather unpacifistic modes of conduct in interpersonal contexts (as opposed to relations with the state).[142]

Pacifism is racist. In displacing massive state violence onto people of color both outside and inside the mother country, rather than absorbing any real measure of it themselves (even when their physical intervention might undercut the state's ability to inflict violence on nonwhites), pacifists can only be viewed as being objectively racist.

Racism itself has been accurately defined as a pathology.[143] Within the context of pacifism, the basic strain must be considered as complicated by an extremely convoluted process of victim blaming under the guise of "antiracism" (a matter linking back to the above-mentioned delusional characteristics of the pathology of pacifism).

Finally, both displacement of violence and victim blaming intertwine in their establishment of a comfort zone for whites who utilize it (perhaps entirely subconsciously) as a basis for "prefiguring" a complex of future "revolutionary" social relations which could serve to largely replicate the present privileged social position of whites vis-à-vis nonwhites as a cultural/intellectual "elite."[144]

The cluster of subparts encompassed by this overall aspect of the pacifist pathology is usually marked by a pronounced tendency on the part of those suffering the illness to react emotionally and with considerable defensiveness to any discussion (in some cases, mere mention) of the nature of racist behaviors. The behavior is typically manifested in agitated assertions—usually with no accusatory finger having been pointed—to the effect that "I have nothing to be ashamed of" or "I have no reason to feel guilty." As with any pathology, this is the proverbial telltale clue indicating s/he is subliminally aware that s/he has much to be ashamed of and is experiencing considerable guilt as a result. Such avoidance may, in extreme cases, merge once again with delusional characteristics of the pathology.[145]

Pacifism is suicidal. In its core impulse to prostrate itself before the obvious reality of the violence inherent in state power, pacifism not only inverts Emiliano Zapata's famous dictum that "It is better to die on one's feet than to live on one's knees"; it actually posits the proposition that is it *best* to die on one's knees and seeks to achieve this result as a matter of *principle*. Pacifist *Eros* is thus transmuted into *Thanatos*.[146]

While it seems certain that at least a portion of pacifism's propensity toward suicide is born of the earlier-mentioned delusion that it can impel nonviolence on the part of the state (and is therefore simply erroneous), there is a likelihood that one of two other factors is at work in many cases:

1. a sublimated death wish manifesting itself in a rather commonly remarked "gambler's neurosis" (i.e., "Can I risk everything and win?").

2. a desublimated death wish manifesting itself in a "political" equivalent of walking out in front of a bus ("Will it hit me or not?").

In any event, this suicidal pathology may be assumed to follow the contours of other such impulses, centering on repressed guilt neuroses and associated feelings of personal inadequacy (in all probability linked to the abovementioned subliminal racism) and severely complicated by a delusional insistence that the death wish itself constitutes a "pro-life" impetus. It is interesting to note that the latter claim has been advanced relative to European Jews during the 1940s.[147]

From even this scanty profile, it is easy enough to discern that pacifism—far from being a praxis adequate to impel revolutionary change—assumes the configuration of a pathological illness when advanced as a political methodology. Given its deep-seated, superficially self-serving, and socially approved nature, it is likely to be an exceedingly difficult pathology to treat and a long-term barrier to the formation of revolutionary consciousness/action in North America. Yet it is a barrier that must be overcome if revolutionary change is to occur, and for this reason we turn to the questions of the nature of the role of nonviolent political action within a viable American transformative praxis, as well as preliminary formulation of a therapeutic approach to the pathology of pacifism.

Toward a Liberatory Praxis

> The variegated canvas of the world is before me; I
> stand over against it; by my theoretical attitude to it I
> overcome its opposition to me and make its contents
> my own. I am at home in the world when I know it,
> still more so when I have understood it.
>
> —G.W.F. Hegel

While standard definitions tend to restrict the meaning of
the term "praxis" to being more or less a sophisticated sub-
stitute for the words "action" or "practice," within the tradition of revolutionary theory it yields a more precise quality.[148]
August von Cieszkowski long ago observed, "Practical philosophy, or more exactly stated, the Philosophy of Praxis,
which could influence life and social relationships, the development of truth in concrete activity—this is the overriding
destiny of philosophy."[149] For Marx, the essence of praxis
lay in the prospect that the ongoing process of changing circumstances (i.e., material conditions) could coincide with a
human self-consciousness which he described as rationally
conceived "self-changing" or "revolutionary praxis."[150] In a
dialectical sense, this entailed a process of qualitative transformation at the level of totality, from practice (relatively
unconscious world-making activity) to praxis (less determined, more conscious world-constituting activity); the distinction between practice and praxis Marx defined as being
between something "in itself" and something "for itself."[151]

Thus, as Richard Kilminster has noted, for Marx:

> The famous "cunning of Reason" in Hegel's *The
> Philosophy of History*[152] "sets of passions" of individuals
> and the collective aspirations of nations "to work for
> itself" in the process of historical self-realization of
> what it essentially is, as comprehended and exempli-
> fied by Reason at its later stages. Strong teleological
> overtones are present in this conception as they are

also in what we might analogously term Marx's implicit notion of a cunning of praxis, through which he discerned history had a consciously appropriable meaning in the blindly developing but ultimately self-rationalizing development of its successive social structures.[153]

In other words, praxis might be accurately defined as action consciously and intentionally guided by theory while simultaneously guiding the evolution of theoretical elaboration. It follows that any liberatory transformation of society is dependent upon the development/articulation of an adequate praxis by which revolutionary struggle may be carried out.[154]

There are a vast range of implications to the praxical symbiosis of theory and practice in prerevolutionary society, most especially within an advanced capitalist context such as that of the United States. To a significant extent, these implications are intellectual/analytical in nature, and the great weight of praxical consideration has correspondingly focused itself in this direction. Insofar as such concerns might rightly be viewed as "strategic," this emphasis is undoubtedly necessary. This is not to say, however, that such preoccupations should be allowed to assume an exclusivist dominance over other matters of legitimate praxical interest. In this regard, the short shrift afforded the more pragmatic or "tactical" aspects of praxis in contemporary dissident theory is, to say the least, disturbing.[155] Such uneven development of praxis is extremely problematic in terms of actualizing revolutionary potential.

A clear example of this tendency may be found in the paucity of recent literature attempting to explore the appropriate *physical* relationship between the repressive/defensive forces of the late capitalist state, on the one hand, and those avowedly pursuing its liberatory transformation, on the other. Little intellectual or practical effort has gone into examining the precise nature of revolutionary (as opposed to ritual) confrontation or the literal requirements of revolutionary struggle within fully industrialized nations. Consequently, a theoretical—hence, praxical—vacuum has appeared in this connection. And, as with any vacuum of this sort, the analytical default has been filled with the most convenient and readily accessible set of operant assumptions available, in this case with pacifism, the doctrine of "revolutionary nonviolence."

Predictably (for reasons already elaborated), the same situation does not prevail with regard to liberatory struggles in the Third World. In terms of both historiography and mythology, it is considered axiomatic that revolution in non-industrialized areas all but *inherently* entails resort to armed struggle and violence.[156] This remains true whether one is considering the Bolshevik revolution, the Chinese revolution, the Vietnamese revolution, the Cuban revolution, the Algerian revolution, decolonization struggles in Africa during the 1950s, the Nicaraguan revolution, the Zimbabwean revolution, or any other.[157] The same principle also holds with regard to Third World liberation movements such as the ANC in South Africa, SWAPO in Namibia, the Tupamaros in Uruguay, Shining Path in Peru, and so on.[158] In each case, the fundamental physical relationship between armed struggle/violence and liberatory posture is clear.

As a matter of praxis, this relationship has been clarified (even codified) by theorists as diverse as Frantz Fanon, Che Guevara, Mao Tse-tung, and Võ Nguyên Giáp, to name but a few.[159] The accuracy of their articulations is so compelling that even such a devout (and principled) North American pacifist as Blase Bonpane has observed that in the Third World, armed struggle is required because "passivity can coexist nicely with repression, injustice, and fascism."[160] Bonpane goes on:

> Unfortunately, we have been brought up on parlor games, where the participants discuss whether or not they are "for" or "against" violence. Can you picture a similar discussion on whether we are for or against disease? Violence, class struggle, and disease are all

> real. They do not go away through mystification. . . .
> Those who deny the reality of violence and class strug-
> gle—like those who deny the reality of disease—are
> not dealing with the real world.[161]

The "real world" of Third World liberatory praxis thus *necessar-ily* incorporates revolutionary violence as an integral element of itself. The principle is also extended to cover certain sit-uations within the less industrialized sectors of the "First World," as is clearly the situation relative to the Spanish Civil War, Irish resistance to British colonial rule, resistance to the Greek Junta during the 1960s and '70s, and—to a certain extent at least—within the context of revolutionary strug-gle in Italy.[162] Hence, only within the most advanced—and privileged—sectors of industrial society is armed struggle/ violence consigned to the "praxical" realm of "counterpro-ductivity," as when the pacifist left queues up to condemn the Black Panther Party, Weatherman, the Red Army Faction (or "Baader-Meinhof Gang," as it was initially called by the reactionary press).[163]

Aside from the obvious moral hypocrisy implicit in this contradiction, the question must be posed as to whether it offers any particular revolutionary advantage to those espous-ing it. Given the availability of self-preserving physical force in the hands of the state, within advanced capitalist contexts no less—or even more—than in colonial/neocolonial situa-tions, the question presents itself "at the bottom line" as an essentially military one.

Within this analytical paradigm, three cardinal tenets and an axiom must be observed. The tenets are: (1) the Napoleonic credo that "victory goes to the side fielding the biggest battalions" (i.e., those exercising the most muscle tend to win contests of force); (2) that sheer scale of force can often be offset through utilization of the element of surprise; and (3) even more than surprise, tactical flexibility (i.e., con-centration of force at weak points) can often compensate for lack of strength or numbers (this is a prime point of jujitsu). The axiom at issue has been adopted as the motto of the British Special Air Service: "Who dares, wins."[164]

The first tenet is, to be sure, a hopeless proposition at the outset of virtually any revolutionary struggle. The "big battalions"—and balance of physical power—inevitably rest with the state's police, paramilitary, and military apparatus, at least through the initial and intermediate stages of the liberatory process. Consequently, Third World revolutionary tacticians have compensated by emphasizing tenets two and three (surprise and flexibility), developing the art of guerrilla warfare to a very high degree.[165] Within the more industrialized contexts of Europe and North America, this has assumed forms typically referred to as "terrorism."[166] In either event, the method has proven increasingly successful in befuddling more orthodox military thinking throughout the twentieth century, has led to a familiar series of fallen dictators and dismantled colonial regimes, and has substantially borne out the thrust of the "dare to struggle, dare to win" axiom.[167]

The hegemony of pacifist activity and thought within the late capitalist states, on the other hand, not only bows before the balance of power that rests with the status quo in any head-on contest by force but also gives up the second and third tenets. With activities self-restricted to a relatively narrow band of ritual forms, pacifist tacticians automatically sacrifice much of their (potential) flexibility in confronting the state; within this narrow band, actions become entirely predictable rather than offering the utility of surprise. The bottom-line balance of physical power thus inevitably rests with the state on an essentially permanent basis, and the possibility of liberal social transformation is correspondingly diminished to a point of nonexistence. The British Special Air Service motto is again borne out, this time via a converse formulation: "Who fails to dare, loses . . . perpetually."

It is evident that whatever the attributes of pacifist doctrine, "revolutionary nonviolence" is a complete misnomer;

pacifism itself offers no coherent praxis for liberatory social transformation. At best, it might be said to yield certain aspects of a viable liberatory praxis, thus assuming the status of a sort of "quasi-praxis." More appropriately, it should be viewed more at the level of ideology termed by Louis Althusser as constituting "Generalities I."[168] As a low level of ideological consciousness (i.e., dogma) rather than the manifestation of a truly praxical outlook, pacifism dovetails neatly with Ernest Gellner's observation that ideological "patterns of legitimacy . . . are first and foremost sets of collectively held beliefs about validity. The psychological ground of legitimacy is in fact the recognition of the validity of a given social norm."[169] Or, to take the matter further, we might turn to the conclusion of J.G. Merquior:

> As far as belief is concerned, ideological legitimacy is chiefly, though not exclusively, for internal consumption. Its function is really to act as a catalyst for the mind of the group whose interest it sublimates into a justificatory set of ideals. Outside the interest-bound class circle, ideology consists primarily of unchallenged, normally tacit, value-orientations which, once translated into the language of purpose, amounts to the "manipulation of bias" in favor of privileged groups. (emphasis in original)[170]

This perception of pacifism as a self-justifying ideological preemption of proper praxical consideration, subliminally intended to perpetuate the privileged status of a given "progressive" elite, is helpful in determining what is necessary to arrive at a true liberatory praxis within advanced capitalist contexts. The all but unquestioned legitimacy accruing to the principles of pacifist practice must be continuously and comprehensively subjected to the test of whether they, in *themselves*, are capable of delivering the bottom-line transformation of state-dominated social relations which alone constitutes the revolutionary/liberatory process.[171] Where they are found to be incapable of such delivery, the principles must be broadened or transcended altogether as a means of achieving an adequate praxis.

By this, it is not being suggested that nonviolent forms of struggle are or should be abandoned, nor that armed struggle should be the normative standard of revolutionary performance, either practically or conceptually. Rather, it is to follow the line of thinking recently articulated by Kwame Ture (Stokely Carmichael) when he noted:

> If we are to consider ourselves as revolutionaries, we must acknowledge that we have an obligation to succeed in pursuing revolution. Here, we must acknowledge not only the power of our enemies, but our own power as well. Realizing the nature of our power, we must not deny ourselves the exercise of the options available to us; we must utilize surprise, cunning, and flexibility; we must use the strength of our enemy to undo him, keeping him confused and off-balance. We must organize with perfect clarity to be utterly unpredictable. When our enemies expect us to respond to provocation with violence, we must react calmly and peacefully; just as they anticipate our passivity, we must throw a grenade.[172]

What is at issue is not therefore the replacement of hegemonic pacifism with some "cult of terror." Instead, it is the realization that in order to be effective and ultimately successful any revolutionary movement within advanced capitalist nations must develop the broadest possible range of thinking/action by which to confront the state. This should be conceived not as an array of component forms of struggle but as a continuum of activity stretching from petitions/letter writing and so forth through mass mobilization/demonstrations onward into the arena of armed self-defense, and still onward through the realm of "offensive" military operations (e.g., elimination of critical state facilities, targeting of key individuals within the governmental/corporate apparatus, etc.).[173] All of this must be apprehended as a holism, as an internally consistent liberatory process applicable at this generally-formulated level to the late capitalist context no less than to the Third World. From the basis of this fundamental understanding—and, it may be asserted, *only* from this basis—can a viable liberatory praxis for North America emerge.

It should by now be self-evident that while a substantial—even preponderant—measure of nonviolent activity is encompassed within any revolutionary praxis, there is no place for the profession of "principled pacifism" to preclude—much less condemn—the utilization of violence as a legitimate and necessary method of achieving liberation. The dismantling of the false consciousness inherent in the ideology of "nonviolent revolution" is therefore of primary importance in attaining an adequate liberatory praxis.

A Therapeutic Approach to Pacifism

> A reversal of perspective is produced vis-à-vis adult consciousness: the historical becoming which prepared it was not before it, it is only for it; the time during which it progressed is no longer the time of its constitution, but a time which it constitutes. . . . Such is the reply of critical thought to psychologism, sociologism and historicism.
>
> —Maurice Merleau-Ponty, 1947

The pervasiveness of "pacifism" within the ostensibly oppositional sectors of American society appear grounded more in a tightly intertwined complex of pathological characteristics than in some well thought through matrix of consciously held philosophical tenets. To the extent that this is true, the extrapolation of pacifist ideological propositions serves to obfuscate rather than clarify matters of praxical concern, to retard rather than further liberatory revolutionary potentials within the United States. Such a situation lends itself more readily to the emergence of a fascist societal construct than to liberatory transformation.[174] Thus, the need to overcome the hegemony of pacifist thinking is clear.

However, as with any pathologically based manifestation, hegemonic pacifism in advanced capitalist contexts proves itself supremely resistant—indeed, virtually impervious—to mere logic and moral suasion. The standard accouterments (such as intelligent theoretical dialogue) of political consciousness raising/movement building have proven relatively useless when confronted within the cynically self-congratulatory obstinacy with which the ideologues of pacifist absolutism defend their faith. What is therefore required as a means of getting beyond the smug exercise of knee-jerk pacifist "superiority" and into the arena of effective liberatory praxis is a therapeutic rather than dialogic approach to the phenomenon.

What follows, then, is a sketch of a strategy by which radical therapists might begin to work through the pacifist problematic in both individual and group settings.[175] It should be noted that the suggested method of approach is contingent upon the therapist's own freedom from contamination with pacifist predilections (it has been my experience that a number of supposed radical therapists are themselves in acute need of therapy in this area).[176] It should also be noted that in the process of elaboration a number of terms from present psychological jargon (e.g., "reality therapy") are simply appropriated for their use value rather than through any formal adherence to the precepts which led to their initial currency. Such instances should be self-explanatory.

Therapy may be perceived as progressing either through a series of related and overlapping stages or phases of indeterminate length.

Values clarification. During this initial portion of the therapeutic process, participants will be led through discussion/consideration of the bases of need for revolutionary social transformation, both objective and subjective. Differentiations between objectively observed and subjectively felt/experienced needs will be examined in depth, with particular attention paid to contradictions—real or perceived—between the two. The outcome of this portion of the process is to assist each participant in arriving at a realistic determination of whether s/he truly holds values consistent with revolutionary aspirations, or whether s/he is not more psychically inclined toward some variant of reforming/modifying the status quo.

The role of the therapist in this setting is to be both extremely conversant with objective factors and to lead subjective responses of participants to an honest correlation in each discursive moment of process. Although this portion of therapy is quite hypothetical/theoretical in nature, it must be anticipated that a significant portion of participants who began defining themselves as pacifists will ultimately adopt a clarified set of personal values of a nonrevolutionary type, that is, acknowledging that they personally wish to pursue a course of action leading to some outcome other than the total transformation of the state/liberation of the most objectively oppressed social sectors.

It would be possible at this point to posit a procedure for attempting the alteration of nonrevolutionary values. However, the purpose of a radical (as opposed to bourgeois) therapy is not to induce accommodation to principles and values other than their own. In the sense that the term is used here, "values clarification" is merely an expedient to calling things by their right names and to strip away superficial/rhetorical layers of delusion.

Reality therapy. Those—including self-defined pacifists— who in the initial phase of the process have coherently articulated their self-concept as being revolutionary will be led into a concrete integration with the physical reality of the objective bases for revolution, as well as application(s) of the revolutionary response to these conditions. This phase is quite multifaceted and contains a broad range of optional approaches.

In short, this second phase of the therapeutic process will include direct and extended exposure to the conditions of life among at least one (and preferably more) of the most objectively oppressed communities in North America, for example, inner-city black ghettos, Mexican and Puerto Rican barrios, American Indian reservations or urban enclaves, Southern rural black communities, and so on. It is expected that participants will not merely "visit" but remain in these communities for extended periods, eating the food, living in comparable facilities, and getting by on the average annual income. Arguments that such an undertaking is unreasonable because it would be dangerous and participants would be unwanted in such communities are not credible; these are the most fundamental reasons *for* going—the reality of existing in perpetual physical jeopardy (and/or of being physically abused in an extreme fashion) precisely *because* of being unwanted (especially on racial grounds), while living in the most squalid of conditions, is precisely what must be understood by self-proclaimed revolutionaries, pacifist or otherwise. Avoiding direct encounters with these circumstances as well as knowledge of them is to avoid revolutionary reality in favor of the comfort zone.

This experience should be followed by a similar sort of exposure to conditions among the oppressed within one or more of the many Third World nations undergoing revolutionary struggle. When at all possible, a part of this process should include linking up directly with one or more of the revolutionary groups operating in that country, a matter which is likely to take time and be dangerous (as will, say, living in an Indian village in Guatemala or Peru). But, again, this is precisely the point; the participant will obtain a clear knowledge of the realities of state repression and armed resistance that cannot be gained in any way other than through direct exposure.

Finally, either during or after the above processes, each participant should engage in some direct and consciously risk-inducing confrontation with state power. This can be done in a myriad of ways, either individually or in a group, but cannot include prior arrangements with police in order to minimize their involvement. Nor can it include obedience to police department demands for "order" once the action begins; participants must adopt a posture of absolute non-cooperation with the state while remaining true to their own declared values (e.g., for pacifists, refraining from violent acts themselves).

The role of the therapist—who should already have such grounding in revolutionary reality him/herself—during this phase of therapy is to facilitate the discussion of the process in both individual and group settings. The therapist must be conversant with the realities being experienced by participants to be able to assist them in establishing and apprehending a proper context in each instance.

Evaluation. For those who complete phase two (and a substantial degree of attrition must be anticipated in association with reality therapy, especially among those who began by espousing nonviolent "alternatives" to armed struggle), there must come a period of independent and guided reflection upon their observations and experiences "in the real world." This can be done on a purely individual basis, but generally speaking, a group setting is best for the guided portion of evaluation. A certain recapitulation/reformulation of the outcomes of the values clarification phase is in order, as is considerable philosophical/situational discussion and analysis coupled to readings; role-play has proven quite effective in many instances.

The point of this portion of the therapeutic process is to achieve a preliminary reconciliation of personal, subjective values with concrete realities. A tangible outcome is obtainable in each participant's formal articulation of precisely how he/she sees his/her values coinciding with the demonstrable physical requirements of revolutionary social action. Again, it should be anticipated that during evaluation a segment of participants will arrive at the autonomous decision that their aspirations/commitments are to something other than revolutionary social transformation.

The role of the therapist during this phase is to serve as a consultant to participant self-evaluation, recommend readings as appropriate to participant concerns/confusions, facilitate role-play and other group dynamics, and assist participants in keeping their reconciliations free of contradictions in logic.

Demystification. It has been my experience that, by this point in the therapeutic process, there are few (if any) remaining participants seeking to extend the principles of pacifist absolutism. And among remaining participants—especially among those who began with such absolutist notions—there often remains a profound lack of practical insight into the technologies and techniques common to both physical repression and physical resistance.

A typical psychological manifestation of such ignorance is the mystification of both the tools at issue and those individuals known to be skilled in their use. For example, a "fear of guns" is intrinsic to the pacifist left, as is sheer irrational terror at the very idea of directly confronting such mythologized characters as members of SWAT teams, Special Forces ("Green Berets"), Rangers, and members of right-wing vigilante organizations. The outcomes of such mystification tend to congeal into feelings of helplessness and inadequacy, rationalization, and avoidance. Sublimated, these feelings reemerge in the form of compensatory rhetoric, attempting to convert low self-confidence into a signification of transcendent virtue (i.e., "make the world go away").

Hence, while few participants will at this juncture be prepared to honestly deny that armed struggle is and must be an integral aspect of the revolutionary interest that they profess to share, a number will still contend that they are "philosophically" unable to directly participate in it. Clarification is obtainable in this connection by bringing out the obvious: knowing how, at some practical level, to engage in armed struggle and then choosing not to is a much different proposition than refraining from such engagement due to ignorance of the means and methods involved.

Here, "hands-on" training and experience is of the essence. The basic technologies at issue—rifles, assault rifles, handguns, shotguns, explosives, and the like, as well as the rudiments of their proper application and deployment—must be explored. This practical training sequence should be augmented and enhanced by selected readings and continual individual and group discussions of the meaning(s) of this new range of skills acquisition.[177]

It should be noted clearly that this phase of therapy is not designed or intended to create "commandos" or to form guerrilla units. Rather, it will serve only to acquaint each participant with the fact that s/he has the same general information/skills base as those who deter him/her through physical intimidation or repression and is at least potentially capable of the same degree of proficiency in these formerly esoteric areas as his/her most "elite" opponents. At this point, nonviolence *can* become a philosophical choice or tactical expedient rather than a necessity born of psychological default.

The role of the therapist during this phase is unlikely to be that of trainer (although it is possible, given that he/she should have already undergone such training). Rather, it is likely to be that of suggesting the appropriate trainers and literature, and serving as discussion/group facilitator for participants.

Reevaluation. In this final phase of therapy, remaining participants will be led into articulation of their overall perspective on the nature and process of revolutionary social transformation (i.e., their understanding of liberatory praxis), including their individual perceptions of their own specific roles within this process. The role of the therapist is to draw each participant out into a full and noncontradictory elaboration, as well as to facilitate the emergence of a potential for future, ongoing reevaluation and development of revolutionary consciousness.

The internal composition of each phase of this therapeutic approach in resolving the problem of hegemonic (pathological) pacifism is open to almost infinite variation on the part of the therapists and participants involved in each instance of application. Even the ordering of phases may be beneficially altered; for example, what has been termed "reality therapy" may have independently preceded and triggered the perceived need for values clarification on the part of some (or many) participants. Or, independently undertaken evaluations may lead some participants to enter values clarification and then proceed to reality therapy. The key for therapists is to retain a sense of flexibility of approach when applying the model, picking up participants at their own points of entry and adapting the model accordingly, rather than attempting some more or less rigid progression.

In sum, it is suggested that the appropriate application of the broad therapeutic model described in this section can have the effect of radically diminishing much of the delusion, the aroma of racism and the sense of privilege which mark the covert self-defeatism accompanying the practice of mainstream dissident politics in contemporary America. At another level—if widely adopted—the model will be of assistance in allowing the construction of a true liberatory praxis, a real "strategy to win," for the first time within advanced industrial society. This potentiality, for those who would claim the mantle of being revolutionary, can only be seen as a positive step.

Conclusion

> In the contradiction lies the hope.
> —Bertolt Brecht

This essay is far from definitive. Its composition and emphasis have been dictated largely by the nature of the dialogue and debate prevailing within the circle of the American opposition today. The main weight of its exposition has gone to critique pacifist thinking and practice; its thrust has been more to debunk the principles of hegemonic nonviolence rather than to posit fully articulated alternatives. In the main, this has been brought about by the degree of resistance customarily thrown up a priori to any challenge extended to the assumption of ontological goodness pacifism accords itself. The examples it raises are intended to at least give pause to those whose answers have been far too pat and whose "purity of purpose" has gone unquestioned for far too long.

A consequence of this has been that the conceptualization of other options, both within this essay and in the society beyond, have suffered. As concerns society, this is an obviously unacceptable situation. As to the essay, it may be asserted that it is to the good. The author is neither vain nor arrogant enough to hold that his single foray could be sufficient to offset the magnitude of problematic issues raised. Instead, it is to be hoped that the emphasis of "Pacifism as Pathology" will cause sufficient anger and controversy that others—many others—will endeavor to seriously address the matters at hand. Within such open and volatile forums, matters of therapeutic and praxical concerns can hopefully advance.

In concluding, I would at last like to state the essential premise of this essay clearly: the desire for a nonviolent and cooperative world is the healthiest of all psychological manifestations. This is the overarching principle of liberation and revolution.[178] Undoubtedly, it seems the highest order of contradiction that, in order to achieve nonviolence, we must first break with it in overcoming its root causes. Therein, however, lies our only hope.

Notes

1   On the matter of alchemy, at least as intended here, see Louis Pauwels and Jacques Bergier, *The Morning of the Magicians* (New York: Stein and Day, 1964) pp. 62–90.

2   V.I. Lenin, *State and Revolution* (New York: International, 1932).

3   The tally of twentieth-century revolutions accomplished through nonviolent means is exactly zero (see the critique of the Gandhian "exception" in the section "An Essential Contradiction").

4   E.g., Committee in Solidarity with the People of El Salvador (CISPES).

5   Probably the best elucidation of the "oppositional praxis" at issue here can be found in Gene Sharp's 902-page trilogy, *The Politics of Nonviolent Action* (Boston: Porter Sargent, 1973), "Part One: Power and Struggle"; "Part Two: The Methods of Nonviolent Action"; and "Part Three: The Dynamic of Nonviolent Action." Meanwhile, on the steady growth of native fascism, see Phillip Finch, *God, Guts and Guns: A Close Look at the Radical Right* (New York: Putnam Adult, 1983); James Coates, *Armed and Dangerous: The Rise of the Survivalist Right* (New York: Noonday, 1987); and Russ Bellant, *Old Nazis, the New Right, and the Republican Party: Domestic Fascist Networks and Their Effect on US Cold War Politics* (Boston: South End Press, 1991).

6   See, e.g., Gene Sharp, *Social Power and Political Freedom* (Boston: Porter Sargent, 1980).

7   Virtually all extant literature on the subject, which is considerable, leaves the same impression on this point. William L. Shirer's *The Rise and Fall of the Third Reich: A History of Nazi Germany* (New York: Simon and Schuster, 1960) still provides as good a capsule view as any single volume. See especially Chapter 27, "The New Order" (pp. 937–94).

8   On this point there are also numerous sources. For example, see Hannah Arendt, *Eichmann in Jerusalem: A Report on the Banality of Evil* (New York: Penguin Books, 1963) pp. 41–48; Heinz Höhne, *The Order of the Death's Head: The Story of Hitler's SS* (New York: Coward-McCann, 1970) pp. 346–47; and Helmut Krausnick, Martin Broszat, and Hans-Adolf Jacobsen, *Anatomy of the SS State* (New York: Walker, 1972) pp. 54–57.

9   Raul Hilberg, *The Destruction of the European Jews* (Chicago: Quadrangle, 1961) pp. 122–25, 297, 316.

10   Isaiah Trunk, *Judenrat: The Jewish Councils in Eastern Europe Under Nazi Occupation* (New York: Macmillan, 1972); Raul Hilberg, "The Judenrat: Conscious or Unconscious Tool?," *Proceedings of the Third Yad Vashem International Historical Conference, 4–7 April 1977* (Jerusalem: Yad Vashem, 1979) pp. 31–44.

11   See Primo Levi, *Survival in Auschwitz: The Nazi Assault on Humanity* (New York: Collier Books, 1961); Miklos Nyiszli, *Auschwitz: A Doctor's Eyewitness Account* (New York: Fawcett Books, 1960); and Terrance Des Pres, *The Survivor: An Anatomy of Life in the Death Camps* (New York: Oxford University Press, 1980).

12   The most careful recent estimates indicate that approximately 5.1 million Jews perished in the Holocaust, 1.1 million in Auschwitz/

Birkenau alone. See Raul Hilberg, *The Destruction of the European Jews*, 3 vols. (New York: Holmes and Meier, [rev. ed.] 1985) Vol. 3, pp. 1047–48, 1201–20. Also see, Franciszek Piper, "The Number of Victims," in Yisrael Gutman and Michael Berenbaum, eds., *Anatomy of the Auschwitz Death Camp* (Bloomington: Indiana University Press, 1994) pp. 61–76.

13   The question is posed in a number of places by various authors. The particular version used here was framed by Bruno Bettelheim on p. ix of his foreword to Nyiszli, *Auschwitz*.

14   Again, the references on this point are quite numerous. As examples, see Hilberg, *Destruction of European Jews*; Martyrs & Heroes Remembrance Authority, *The Holocaust* (Jerusalem, Palestine: Yad Vashem, 1975); and Irving Louis Horowitz, *Genocide: State Power and Mass Murder* (New Brunswick, NJ: Transaction Books, 1976).

15   E.g., Yehuda Bauer and Nathan Rotenstreich, eds., *The Holocaust as Historical Experience: Essays and Discussion* (New York: Holmes and Meier, 1981).

16   But not, as assorted zionist propagandists such as Yehuda Bauer, Deborah Lipstadt, Emil Fackenheim, Lucy Dawidowicz, and Steven T. Katz would have it, to a degree unique in all history. Slavs, Gypsies, homosexuals, and leftists shared a similar fate under nazi rule. Approximately two-thirds of Europe's Jews were exterminated by the nazis, while at least the same percentage (and probably more) of all North American Indians were "extirpated" by the United States and its colonial antecedents. The butchery of Armenians by Turks in 1915 also rivals the Holocaust in intensity, if not in scale, as does the genocide of East Timorese by Indonesia between 1975 and 1977, and—in some respects—the treatment accorded Palestinians by Israel today. See generally Bohdan Wytwycky, *The Other Holocaust: Many Circles of Hell: A Brief Account of the 9–10 Million Persons Who Died with 6 Million Jews Under Nazi Racism* (Washington, DC: Novak Report on the New Ethnicity, 1980); Frank Chalk and Kurt Jonassohn, *The History and Sociology of Genocide: Analyses and Case Studies* (New Haven: Yale University Press, 1990); Michael Berenbaum, ed., *A Mosaic of Victims: Non-Jews Persecuted and Murdered by the Nazis* (New York: New York University Press, 1990); and Alan S. Rosenbaum, ed., *Is the Holocaust Unique? Perspectives on Comparative Genocide* (Boulder, CO: Westview Press, 1996).

17   Actually, to be fair, such accusations transcend zionism. A classic example occurred during the preparation of this manuscript. It was sent out for review and comments to a Denver-based antizionist Jewish organization, which was sharply critical of the use of the Holocaust to illustrate many of the points made herein. The very

first objection raised was that using "'Like Lambs to the Slaughter' as a heading is just asking to be called antisemitic, especially since the argument does not reflect the facts." Interestingly, among the materials sent along to "correct" my factual understanding of the extent and effectiveness of Jewish armed resistance to the Holocaust was a xeroxed excerpt from Lucy Dawidowicz's *War Against the Jews, 1933–1945* (New York: Holt, Rinehart and Winston, 1975) containing the following passage at p. 423: "The only question facing the Jews [announced a zionist leader in 1943] was how to choose to die: 'either like sheep for the slaughter or like men of honor.' Among the Zionist youth in the resistance movement, 'like sheep for the slaughter' became an epithet of ignominy, divorced from its original [Hebraic] meaning of martyrdom. These young Zionists, in their statements and proclamations, [expressed] a feeling of anger against Jewish passivity." I may perhaps be forgiven for observing that this is *exactly* the argument I've been making. One can accept it or reject it, but one cannot do both at once (as my critics seek to do). And, to label as "antisemitic" the application of an explicitly Jewish phrase to a context and in a fashion in which it has already been emphatically applied by Jews? Unto me giveth a break. This is not constructive criticism. Rather, it is the use of name-calling and factual distortion to foreclose on inconvenient discussion. One solace is that being subjected to such nonsense places me in some pretty good company; Jewish scholars like Hannah Arendt, Raul Hilberg, and Arno J. Mayer have suffered similar indignities at the hands of their own community after raising comparably uncomfortable issues with respect to the Judaic response to nazism; see Dwight Macdonald, "Hannah Arendt and the Jewish Establishment," *Partisan Review*, XXXI (1964) pp. 262–69 ; on Hilberg, see Michael R. Marrus, "Jewish Resistance to the Holocaust," *Journal of Contemporary History*, Vol. 30, No. 1 (January 1995) pp. 83–110; and Arno J. Mayer, "Memory and History: On the Poverty of Remembering and Forgetting the Judeocide," *Radical History Review*, No. 56 (Spring 1993) pp. 5–20. For further, and entirely cogent, consideration of the "like sheep to the slaughter" phenomenon and its implications, see Robert G. L. Waite, "The Holocaust and Historical Explanation," in Isidor Wallimann and Michael N. Dobkowski, eds., *Genocide and the Modern Age: Etiology and Case Studies of Mass Death* (Westport, CT: Greenwood Press, 1987) pp. 163–84.

18   Bettelheim, foreword to Nyiszli's *Auschwitz*, p. xiv.

19   It should be noted that similar revolts in Sobibór and Treblinka in 1943 were even more effective than the one at Auschwitz/Birkenau a few months later; Sobibór had to be closed altogether, a reality

which amplifies and reinforces Bettelheim's rather obvious point. See Miriam Novitch, *Sobibór: Martyrdom and Revolt* (New York: Holocaust Library, 1980); Jean-François Steiner, *Treblinka* (New York: Simon and Schuster, 1967); and Yisrael Gutman, "Rebellions in the Camps: Three Revolts in the Face of Death," in Alex Grobman and Daniel Landes, eds., *Genocide, Critical Issues of the Holocaust* (Los Angeles: Simon Wiesenthal Center, 1983) pp. 256–60.

20   Bettelheim, foreword to Nyiszli's *Auschwitz*, p. xi.

21   Ibid., p. vi. Similar observations have been made by others, notably Raul Hilberg in the 1985 edition of *The Destruction of the European Jews* (Teaneck, NJ: Holmes & Meier Publishers, [2nd ed.] 1985); and Arno J. Mayer, in his *Why Did the Heavens Not Darken? The "Final Solution" in History* (New York: Pantheon Books, [rev. ed.] 1990).

22   Bettelheim, foreword to Nyiszli's *Auschwitz*, p. viii.

23   A succinct overview of the Nuremberg Laws and related pieces of nazi legislation can be found in Stefan Kuhl, *The Nazi Connection: Eugenics, American Racism, and German National Socialism* (New York: Oxford University Press, 1994) pp. 73, 97–98.

24   Bettelheim, foreword to Nyiszli's *Auschwitz*, p. x.

25   Ibid.

26   It is apprehension of precisely this point, whether concretely or intuitively, which seems to be guiding a school of revisionism which seeks to supplant images of the passivity of the preponderance of Jews during the Holocaust with a rather distorted impression that armed resistance to nazism was pervasive among this victim group. Probably the definitive effort in this connection is Reuben Ainsztein's massive *Jewish Resistance in Nazi-Occupied Eastern Europe: With a Historical Survey of the Jew as Fighter and Soldier in the Diaspora* (New York: Barnes and Noble, 1974). Other noteworthy contributions to the literature in this respect include Isaiah Trunk's *Jewish Responses to Nazi Persecution: Collective and Individual Behavior in Extremis* (New York: Stein and Day, 1979); and Yehuda Bauer's "Jewish Resistance and Passivity in the Face of the Holocaust," in François Furet, ed., *Unanswered Questions: Nazi Germany and the Genocide of the Jews* (New York: Schocken Books, 1989) pp. 235–51. These efforts, and others like them, perform an admirable service in fleshing out the woefully incomplete record of Jewish resistance—and perhaps to counter notions that Jewish passivity resulted from congenital or cultural "cowardice," misimpressions which should never have held currency anyway—but they do nothing to render the extent of Jewish armed struggle greater than it was. Arguments to the contrary—such as that advanced by the critics mentioned in note 17 are purely polemical (or emotional).

27   This "spiritual dimension" has in fact been one of the major the-
     matics of the most noted analysts of the meaning of the Holocaust,
     Elie Wiesel. See Alvin H. Rosenfeld and Irving Greenberg, eds.,
     Confronting the Holocaust: The Impact of Elie Wiesel (Bloomington:
     Indiana University Press, 1978).

28   As to the implications of the disarmed and therefore utterly unpre-
     pared state of the Jewish resistance in its efforts to formulate an
     adequate response to the nazis, see Bauer, "Resistance and Passivity,"
     pp. 240–41.

29   For a taste of such reasoning, see David Garrow's Pulitzer Prize–
     winning *Bearing the Cross: Martin Luther King Jr., and the Southern Christian
     Leadership Conference* (New York: William Morrow, 1986).

30   This is the premise advanced in works such as Joan V. Bondurant's
     The Conquest of Violence: The Gandhian Philosophy of Conflict (Berkeley:
     University of California Press, 1973).

31   Lesser insurrections "took place in Kruszyna, Krychow, and Lublin
     prisoner-of-war camp, the Kopernikus camp at Mińsk-Mazowiecki,
     at Sachsenhausen, and perhaps elsewhere"; Bauer, "Resistance and
     Passivity," p. 243.

32   For an excellent account of the only recorded mass Jewish armed
     resistance to extermination, see Emmanuel Ringelblum, *Notes
     from the Warsaw Ghetto: The Journal of Emmanuel Ringelblum* (New
     York: McGraw-Hill, 1958). A much smaller ghetto revolt occurred
     in Białystok in August 1943. Additionally, there were "three armed
     revolts [and] four attempted rebellions" in ghettos in the Polish
     General Government area during 1942–1943. See Bauer, "Resistance
     and Passivity," pp. 241–42.

33   Again, to be fair, it wasn't just the SS, a point made long ago by
     Gerald Reitlinger in his *The SS: Alibi of a Nation, 1922–1945* (New
     York: Viking Press, 1957). Aside from this exterminatory elite,
     large numbers of rather common Germans participated volun-
     tarily and with enthusiasm in the Final Solution; see Christopher
     R. Browning, *Ordinary Men: Reserve Police Battalion 101 and the Final
     Solution in Poland* (New York: HarperCollins, 1992). Indeed, there
     is substantial evidence that a majority of Germans knew of and to
     varying extents endorsed the nazi judeocide; John Weiss, *Ideology of
     Death: Why the Holocaust Happened in Germany* (Chicago: Ivan R. Dee,
     1996).

34   See generally Hilberg, *Destruction of the European Jews*; and Dawidowicz,
     War Against the Jews.

35   See generally Henry L. Feingold, *The Politics of Rescue: The Roosevelt
     Administration and the Holocaust, 1938–1945* (New Brunswick, NJ:
     Rutgers University Press, 1970).

36 See Moshe Pearlman, *The Capture and Trial of Adolf Eichmann: The History of Israel's Abduction and Execution of the Holocaust's Architect* (New York: Simon and Schuster, 1963). For the quote paraphrased, see Edward W. Knappmann, "The Adolf Eichmann Trial, 1961," in his *Great World Trials* (Detroit: Gale Research, 1997) p. 335.

37 Quoted in Arendt, *Eichmann in Jerusalem*, p. 17.

38 Arguably, the slogan pertains to judeocide rather than genocide, as such. See Ronald Aronson, "Never Again? Zionism and the Holocaust," *Social Text*, No. 3 (Autumn 1980) pp. 60–72.

39 Gandhi himself is rather candid about this, as is evidenced in his autobiographical *All Men Are Brothers* (New York: Continuum, 1982).

40 For an adequate assessment of this factor, see Alan Campbell-Johnson, *Mission with Mountbatten* (London: Robert Hale, 1951) pp. 119–34.

41 Louis Fischer, *The Life of Mahatma Gandhi* (New York: Harper, 1950), especially Chap. II; Leo Kuper, *Passive Resistance in South Africa* (New Haven, CT: Yale University Press, 1957). This reality is noticeably different from that claimed for the Mahatma by his adherents from very early on. See, e.g., Krishnala Shridharani, *War Without Violence: A Study of Gandhi's Method and Its Accomplishments* (New York: Harcourt Brace, 1939).

42 An excellent assessment of the early relationship between SNCC and King's main organization, the Southern Christian Leadership Conference, can be found in Howard Zinn, *SNCC: The New Abolitionists* (Boston: Beacon Press, 1967). On their increasing divergence on political/tactical issues, see Clayborne Carson, *In Struggle: SNCC and the Black Awakening of the 1960s* (Cambridge, MA: Harvard University Press, 1981) pp. 191–228; on the 1969 change from "Nonviolent" to "National," see p. 296.

43 H. Rap Brown's *Die Nigger Die! A Political Autobiography* (New York: Dial, 1969) contains a very lucid elaboration of the context of Black Power. Also see Robert F. Williams, *Negroes with Guns* (Chicago: Third World Press, 1962); Stokely Carmichael and Charles V. Hamilton, *Black Power: The Politics of Liberation in America* (New York: Random House, 1967); Nathan Wright Jr., *Black Power and Urban Unrest* (New York: Hawthorn, 1967); Julius Lester, *Look Out, Whitey! Black Power's Gon' Get Your Mama!* (New York: Dial, 1968).

44 Or most of it, anyway. It is clear that FBI Director J. Edgar Hoover continued to manifest a virulent hatred of King personally, using the power of his agency in a relentless effort to destroy the civil rights leader. Rather murkier is the possibility that the bureau participated in orchestrating King's 1968 assassination. See David J. Garrow, *The FBI and Martin Luther King Jr.: From "Solo" to Memphis* (New York: W. W.

Norton, 1981). Also see Mark Lane and Dick Gregory, *Code Name "Zorro": The Assassination of Dr. Martin Luther King Jr.* (Englewood Cliffs, NJ: Prentice-Hall, 1977); William F. Pepper, *Orders to Kill: The Truth Behind the Murder of Martin Luther King* (New York: Carroll & Graf, 1995), especially pp. 141–42, 223, 231, 260, 294–95.

45 The provision, inserted into the 1968 Civil Rights Act (82 Stat. 73 § 2201) by paleoconservative senator Strom Thurmond, made it a federal felony to cross state lines "with intent to incite riot." While enforcement of many of the Act's ostensibly affirmative provisions has languished, the "antiriot" provision was immediately applied with vigor in an effort to neutralize what authorities perceived as the leadership of an array of dissident organizations. See, e.g., Jason Epstein, *The Great Conspiracy Trial: An Essay on Law, Liberty and the Constitution* (New York: Random House, 1970).

46 Even the title of King's last book, *Where Do We Go From Here: Chaos or Community?* (New York: Bantam, 1967), suggests he was consciously using the existence of an armed or "violent" trend among politicized American blacks as a foil against which to further the objectives of his own nonviolent movement. In other words, without a number of his ostensible constituents "picking up the gun," King was rendered rather less effective in pursuit of his own pacifist politics.

47 It can, of course, be pointed out that the Jews really constituted no threat at all to the nazi state, and that assertions to the contrary (especially genocidal ones) were/are ridiculously irrational. True. However, this does nothing to disrupt the logic or structure of the situation. The fact is that nazi theoreticians and policy makers *perceived* the Jews as a threat, and their programs were formulated accordingly. As Robert Cecil demonstrates compellingly in *The Myth of the Master Race: Alfred Rosenberg and Nazi Ideology* (New York: Dodd, Mead, 1972), the nazis really did believe, among other things, in the existence of a "Red (communist), Black (anarchist) and Gold (banker) Conspiracy" of Jews which they were duty bound to eradicate. The fact that their exercise of state power was in this respect utterly irrational did nothing to alter the fact of that power or to save one Jew from the effects of it. Nor is the situation as aberrant as it might first appear; the reader is invited to compare the virulence of nazi antisemitism during the pregenocidal 1930s to the nature of official U.S. anticommunism, especially during the McCarthy era. This is but one parallel.

48 As concerns Gandhi's particular windfall(s), see Peter Ward Fey, *The Forgotten Army: India's Armed Struggle for Independence, 1942–1945* (Ann Arbor: University of Michigan Press, 1993).

49 An interesting study in this connection is Mark Calloway's aptly titled *Heavens on Earth: Utopian Communities in America, 1680–1880* (New

York: Dover, 1966). It will be observed that each pacifist "prefigura-tion" of a broader social application proved an abject failure (this is as distinct from the much more sustained—but completely insular—employment of many of the same principles by religious communities such as the Amish).

50   On the nature and magnitude of suffering at issue in Latin America alone, see, e.g., Fidel Castro's "Second Declaration of Havana (February 4, 1962)," included in Martin Kenner and James Petras, eds., *Fidel Castro Speaks* (New York: Grove Press, 1969) pp. 93–117; see especially p. 111.

51   More than a thousand were killed in the Jallianwala Bagh massacre alone, while some 14,000 were jailed during the 1942 *satyagraha* cam-paign. See generally Francis G. Hutchins, *India's Revolution: Gandhi and the Quit India Movement* (Cambridge, MA: Harvard University Press, 1973).

52   See, e.g., Seth Cagin and Philip Dray, *We Are Not Afraid: The Story of Goodman, Schwerner and Chaney and the Civil Rights Campaign for Mississippi* (New York: Macmillan, 1988).

53   A succinct but comprehensive elaboration of the literal context in which the self-immolations occurred may be found in Michael Maclear, *The Ten Thousand Day War: Vietnam, 1945–1975* (New York: St. Martin's Press, 1981); on the monks, see pp. 63–64; on Morrison, see p. 143. For assessment of the media context, see Todd Gitlin, *The Whole World Is Watching: Mass Media in the Making and Unmaking of the New Left* (Berkeley: University of California Press, 1980).

54   If, as has been plausibly suggested, the monks' real agenda was more to eliminate the Diệm regime than American presence per se, their campaign must be assessed as rather more successful than would otherwise be the case. Largely as a result of the furor and negative PR image generated in the United States by the self-immolations and Saigon's utterly callous response, Diệm was ousted in a coup d'état on the night of November 1–2, 1963. It should be noted, however, that the coup was accomplished by the military and in an emphatically violent fashion—Diệm and his brother Nhu were assassinated—an outcome which is hardly pacifist. See Stanley Karnow, *Vietnam: A History* (New York: Penguin, 1984) pp. 206–39.

55   See Jack Nelson and Ronald J. Ostrow, *The FBI and the Berrigans: The Making of a Conspiracy* (New York: Coward, McCann & Geoghegan, 1972).

56   See, e.g., Holly Sklar, *Washington's War on Nicaragua* (Boston: South End Press, 1999) pp. 161, 349.

57   See Robert Hunter, *Warriors of the Rainbow: A Chronicle of the Greenpeace Movement* (New York: Holt, Rinehart and Winston, 1979); Susan

Zakin, *Coyotes and Town Dogs: Earth First! and the Environmental Movement* (New York: Viking, 1993); and Judi Bari, *Timber Wars* (Monroe, ME: Common Courage, 1994).

58 Let's be clear on this point: "revolution" means to obliterate the existing status quo and replace it with something else, not to engage in reformist efforts to render it "better" while leaving it in place. Revolution thus implies a fundamental rejection of things as they are; reform implies a fundamental acceptance.

59 For an amusing summary of this trend, see David Zane Mairowitz, *The Radical Soap Opera: An Impression of the American Left from 1917 to the Present* (London: Wildwood House, 1974).

60 The principles are laid out clearly in Bradford Lyttle's *The Importance of Discipline in Demonstrations for Peace* (New York: Committee for Nonviolent Action, 1962). Abbie Hoffman does a good job of analyzing this phenomenon in his *Revolution for the Hell of It* (New York: Dial Press, 1968). More broadly, see New Yippie Book Collective, eds., *Blacklisted News: Secret History from Chicago to 1984* (New York: Bleecker, 1983).

61 Excellent elaborations concerning police functions can be found in Lynn Cooper, et al., *The Iron First and the Velvet Glove: An Analysis of U.S. Police* (Berkeley: Center for Research on Criminal Justice, 1975) and David Wise, *The American Police State: The Government Against the People* (New York; Random House, 1976).

62 At another level, see the critique offered by Daniel Cohn-Bendit of the Communist Party's collaboration to the same end with the Gaullist government during the 1968 French student/worker uprising in his *Obsolete Communism: The Left-Wing Alternative* (New York: McGraw-Hill, 1968).

63 See Herbert Marcuse, "Repressive Tolerance," in Robert Paul Wolff, Barrington Moore Jr., and Herbert Marcuse, *A Critique of Pure Tolerance* (Boston: Beacon Press, 1969) pp. 81–117; see especially pp. 101–2.

64 See "Elevating Moderating Alternatives: The Moment of Reform," in Gitlin, *The Whole World Is Watching*, pp. 205–32.

65 *New Left Notes* (June–July 1968).

66 For an excellent overall sampling of the more professional efforts at such advertising, see *Images of an Era: The American Poster, 1945–75* (Washington, DC: National Collection of Fine Arts, Smithsonian Institution, 1975). Also see Mitchell Goodman, ed., *The Movement Toward a New America: The Beginnings of a Long Revolution* (Philadelphia/New York: Pilgrim/Alfred A. Knopf, 1970).

67 See Barbara Epstein, "The Politics of Symbolic Protest," *Redline* (March 1988).

68   What is at issue is an altogether different matter from the identically named training delivered to SNCC volunteers prior to their going "on line" in locales like rural Mississippi in the early 1960s. The SNCC training was designed to provide survival skills in the face of the virtual certainty that volunteers would suffer vicious physical assaults from the police while its supposed equivalent in the 1980s and '90s is predicated on the opposite expectation. On the nature and assumptions of SNCC training, see Carson, *In Struggle*. The same general rule applies to the kind of instruction provided by the Revolutionary Youth Movement/Weatherman wing of SDS; Kathy Boudin, Brian Glick, and Gustin Reichbach, *The Bust Book: What to Do Until the Lawyer Comes* (New York: Grove Press, 1969).

69   A prime example is that of the annual protests of nuclear weapons testing in Nevada during the 1980s. This is well covered in Rebecca Solnit's *Savage Dreams: A Journey into the Hidden Wars of the American West* (San Francisco: Sierra Club Books, 1994).

70   E.g., during a carefully orchestrated protest of the annual Columbus Day celebration in 1990, Russell Means, a leader of the American Indian Movement of Colorado, poured a gallon of imitation blood over a statue of the "Great Discoverer" in the city's central plaza. (He was thereupon issued a citation for "desecrating a venerated object.") Ultimately, in forcing the cancellation of the Columbus Day event by 1992—the 500th anniversary of the Columbian landfall—Colorado AIM used every nonviolent tactic mentioned in this section. What separates AIM's stance from that of the entities critiqued in this essay is that its strategy has never foreclosed upon armed struggle. To the contrary, it has consistently employed the latter as and when such methods have seemed appropriate. Hence, its strategic posture evidences the full continuum of tactical options.

71   For a panoramic overview, see Barbara Epstein, *Political Protest and Cultural Revolution: Nonviolent Direct Action in the 1970s and 1980s* (Berkeley: University of California Press, 1991).

72   Consider, for example, the perfectly orderly mass arrests of more than 500 individuals protesting CIA recruitment on the University of Colorado's Boulder campus in 1985. No bail was required, and no cases were prosecuted. Instead, some arrestees were known to frame their "obstruction" citations in the same manner that they might other honors, awards, and diplomas. CIA recruitment, incidentally, continues at the institution more than a decade later.

73   There are, of course, exceptions, as when a group of pacifists from Silo Plowshares managed to get into a nuclear weapons compound near Chicago during the early 1980s and attempted to disable several

missiles. The potential efficacy of this technique—as opposed to holding "vigils" outside the facility's gates—caused the government to make "deterrent examples" of the "culprits." The offending Plowshares activists were promptly labeled "terrorists"—a matter which shows clearly that political effectiveness rather than use of violence is the defining characteristic underlying official use of the term—and two of them were subsequently incarcerated in the federal "supermaximum" prison at Marion, Illinois, for several years. So outrageous was the government's distortion of the facts in this case that at least one veteran FBI agent, John Ryan, resigned rather than participate in the frame-up. See "Once a G-Man, Now a Pacifist: A Costly Conversion," *Newsweek* (November 23, 1987).

74   Again, there are always exceptions (which, of course, simply prove the rule). The Plowshares case mentioned in the preceding note is salient. The leadership of the AIM protests mentioned in note 70 were prosecuted with the intent that they suffer a year's imprisonment. For another good illustration, see Daniel Berrigan, *The Trial of the Catonsville Nine* (Boston: Beacon Press, 1970).

75   Former U.S. Defense Secretary Robert S. McNamara, in an interview on *Larry King Live* (May 1996), placed the overall tally of Indochinese corpses at 3.2 million. On Chile, see Jorge Palacios, *Chile: An Attempt at "Historic Compromise"* (Chicago: Banner, 1979). On El Salvador, see Maria Teresa Tula, *Hear My Testimony* (Boston: South End Press, 1994). On Guatemala, see Edward R.F. Sheehan, *Agony in the Garden: A Stranger in Guatemala* (New York: Houghton Mifflin, 1989). On Grenada, see Edwin P. Hoyt, *America's Wars and Military Incursions* (New York: McGraw-Hill, 1987) pp. 531–45. On Panama, see the Independent Commission of Inquiry on the U.S. Invasion of Panama, *The U.S. Invasion of Panama: The Truth Behind Operation "Just Cause"* (Boston: South End Press, 1991). On Nicaragua, see Holly Sklar, *Washington's War on Nicaragua*. On the Gulf war, see Cynthia Peters, ed., *Collateral Damage: The "New World Order" at Home and Abroad* (Boston: South End Press, 1992).

76   For a comprehensive study of such "overlooked" matters as the U.S.-supported Indonesian genocide in East Timor, circa 1975–77, see Noam Chomsky and Edward S. Herman, *The Political Economy of Human Rights*, 2 vols. (Boston: South End Press, 1979). Also see A.J. Langguth, *Hidden Terrors: The Truth About U.S. Police Operations in Latin America* (New York: Pantheon Books, 1978) for an in-depth examination of such things on a hemispheric basis. William Blum's *Killing Hope: U.S. Military and CIA Interventions Since World War II* (Monroe, ME: Common Courage Press, 1995) will round out the picture through the end of the 1980s. Daniel P. Bolger's *Savage Peace: Americans at War*

in the 1990s (San Francisco: Presidio Press, 1995) will help fill in gaps
for the early 1990s.

77   In her autobiography, *Growing Up Underground* (New York: William
      Morrow, 1981), Jane Alpert offers vivid recollections of her fear that
      nonviolent "allies" would turn her in to the police should her identity
      as a fugitive bomber of corporate targets become known to them.
      Her "paranoia" was justified by the probability that Weather fugi-
      tives such as Cathy Wilkerson had already been apprehended on
      the basis of tips to the police provided by pacifists with "principled
      objections to Weatherman's political violence." For an amazingly
      candid (if unintended) profession of support for the police vis-à-
      vis armed oppositional cadres by a "pacifist feminist," see Ellen
      Frankfort, *Kathy Boudin and the Dance of Death* (New York: Stein and
      Day, 1983). That Frankfort's incredibly racist and reactionary views
      are widely shared, at least among pacifist feminists, is evidenced by
      the excellent reviews her book received. The whole squalid trend
      probably culminated with publication of Robin Morgan's *The Demon
      Lover: On the Sexuality of Terrorism* (New York: W. W. Norton, 1989).

78   David Dellinger, "The Bread Is Rising," in Michael Albert and David
      Dellinger, eds., *Beyond Survival: New Directions for the Disarmament
      Movement* (Boston: South End Press, 1983) p. 33. One is at a loss as to
      what to make of such a statement. How does he know such a program
      would be counterproductive, given support rather than obstruction
      by people like him? Such a context, after all, has never been evident
      in the United States. Further, Dellinger has often been quite vocal in
      his support for armed struggle *elsewhere* (e.g., the National Liberation
      Front in Vietnam). Could it be that he perceives resort to arms to be
      more viable when other than American activists will do the fighting?
      For further insight, see Dellinger's *Vietnam Revisited: Covert Action to
      Invasion to Reconstruction* (Boston: South End Press, 1986).

79   Sam Brown, "Statement to the Associated Press" (December 5,
      1969). It is perhaps indicative of Brown's notion of the importance
      of symbolic rather than concrete actions against the government
      he claimed to oppose that he shortly thereafter accepted a position
      working in it. It simply wouldn't do to disrupt the functioning of
      one's future employer, after all. The nature of Brown's own com-
      mitment can be readily contrasted to those he dismissed as "scruffy"
      in that many of them ultimately went underground and/or to prison
      in pursuit of their beliefs. On Brown's post-Moratorium career, see
      Senate Record Vote Analysis (Washington, DC: 103rd Cong., 2d
      Sess., May 24, 1994), Vote No. 131, Nomination of Sam W. Brown Jr.,
      for the Rank of Ambassador during his tenure of service as Head
      of Delegation to the Conference on Security and Cooperation in

Europe, online at http://www.senate.gov/legislative/LIS/roll_call_
lists/roll_call_vote_cfm.cfm?congress=103&session=2&vote=00131.

80   Ken Hurwitz, *Marching Nowhere* (New York: W. W. Norton, 1971).

81   Davis, who'd been one of the eight defendants in the 1969–70
     Chicago conspiracy trial, was by 1971 speaking on behalf of an SDS
     offshoot calling itself the "May Day Tribe." For a surprisingly accu-
     rate summary of his political evolution, see Gitlin, *The Whole World
     Is Watching*, pp. 167–70.

82   See, e.g., Doug Jenness, "Mass Action versus Calculated
     Confrontation: An Answer to the May Day Tribe," *The Militant* (April
     30, 1971) p. 9; Mairowitz, *Radical Soap Opera*, pp. 221–26.

83   The best description of this development is found in Kirkpatrick
     Sale, *SDS: The Rise and Development of the Students for a Democratic Society*
     (New York: Vintage, 1974) pp. 455–600. A contending (and erro-
     neous) thesis is offered in Alan Adelson, *SDS: A Profile* (New York:
     Charles Scribner's Sons, 1972) pp. 225–70.

84   See Michael Lerner, "Weatherman: The Politics of Despair," in
     Harold Jacobs, ed., *Weatherman* (Berkeley: Ramparts Press, 1970)
     pp. 400–421.

85   Perhaps the preeminent topical articulation of this defection—
     an obvious precursor to the sort of swill later produced by Ellen
     Frankfort and Robin Morgan (note 77)—accrues from another white
     feminist, Gail Sheehy, in her *Panthermania: The Clash of Black Against
     Black in One American City* (New York: Harper & Row, 1971).

86   For details, see Jo Durden-Smith, *Who Killed George Jackson: Fantasies,
     Paranoia and the Revolution* (New York: Alfred A. Knopf, 1976); Huey P.
     Newton, *War Against the Panthers: A Study of Repression in America* (New
     York/London: Harlem River Press, 1996); Ward Churchill and Jim
     Vander Wall, *The COINTELPRO Papers: Documents from the FBI's Secret
     Wars Against Dissent in the United States* (Boston: South End Press, 1990),
     especially pp. 91–164.

87   There is nothing at all metaphorical intended by this statement.
     Leaving aside the obvious holocaust embodied in the institution-
     alization of slavery prior to the Civil War. See, e.g., Herbert Shapiro,
     White Violence and Black Response: From Reconstruction to Montgomery
     (Amherst: University of Massachusetts Press, 1988). For further back-
     ground, see Stewart E. Tolnay and E. M. Beck, *A Festival of Violence: An
     Analysis of Southern Lynchings, 1882–1930* (Athens: University of Georgia
     Press, 1992) and W. Fitzhugh Brundage, *Lynching in the New South:
     Georgia and Virginia, 1880–1930* (Urbana: University of Illinois Press,
     1993).

88   Irv Kurki, speech to the Bradley University Peace Congress, Peoria,
     Illinois, December 12, 1969. Kurki was at the time director of

the local draft counseling office in Peoria and downstate Illinois organizer for the Resistance organization. His views in this regard were voiced in the wake of the December 4, 1969, assassination of Illinois Panther leaders Fred Hampton and Mark Clark (head of the Party's Peoria chapter) in Chicago. The sentiments are shared in Sheehy's *Panthermania* and elsewhere. For the best elaboration of what was known at the time about police operations to neutralize Hampton and the Party more generally—and, consequently, the extent to which statements such as Kurki's add up to conscious victim blaming—see Roy Wilkins and Ramsey Clark et al., *Search and Destroy: A Report by the Commission of Inquiry into the Black Panthers and the Police* (New York: Metropolitan Applied Research Center, 1973). Further examination of the psychology involved will be found in William Ryan, *Blaming the Victim* (New York: Vintage Books, 1971).

89 There can be no question that the magnitude of slaughter in Indochina was known by American nonviolent oppositionists, even as it was occurring. See, e.g., David Dellinger, "Unmasking Genocide," *Liberation* (December 1967/January 1968) p. 3. Given this understanding, which undeniably equates the posture of the U.S. government with that of the Third Reich, at least in some key respects, the pacifist response to the war in Indochina was tantamount to arguing that the appropriate response to nazism was not physical resistance. See again the above sections of this essay devoted to the implications of any such attitude on the part of those targeted for extermination.

90 For another example—this one concerning nineteenth-century white immigrant anarchists framed by police provocateurs in Chicago and subsequently executed by the State of Illinois—see Bradford Lyttle, *Haymarket: Violence Destroys a Movement* (New York: Committee for Nonviolent Action, 1965). For the reality of what occurred—rather than Lyttle's patently victim-blaming version of it—see Henry David, *History of the Haymarket Affair* (New York: Collier, 1963).

91 Fanon addresses this aspect of displacement in a section titled "French Intellectuals and Democrats and the Algerian Revolution," in his *Toward the African Revolution* (New York: Grove Press, 1968) pp. 76–90.

92 In this sense, the term "responsible" should be considered as interchangeable with "respectable." Neither term is self-explanatory, although they are invariably employed as if they were. The relevant questions which should always be posed when such characterizations come up are "responsible to *what*?" and "respected by *whom*?"

93 "Radical movements" which devote themselves to liberally sanctioned causes like First Amendment rights, including those which

appear temporarily most vibrant and energetic, are ultimately self-coopting and diversionary in terms of real social issues. Their "victories," in and of themselves, tend to reinforce rather than erode the functioning of the status quo. For a classic illustration, see David Lance Goines, *The Free Speech Movement: Coming of Age in the 1960s* (Berkeley: Ten Speed Press, 1993).

94   This is standard form in a liberal democracy, no matter how "conservative" its garb. See Thomas I. Emerson, *The System of Freedom of Expression* (New York: Random House, 1970).

95   An even more sophisticated approach was taken by West German counterterrorism expert Christian Lochte in his advocacy of factoring a certain (containable) quantity of violence by the opposition into elite calculations of the costs of maintaining the status quo. His point was that the functioning of the modem state inherently generates such responses, and at least tacit support of them across a fairly wide spectrum of the public. By absorbing an "acceptable" level of activity by small clandestine groups like the Red Army Faction without reacting in an overly repressive fashion, he argued, the state security apparatus could fashion a useful sociopolitical venting mechanism which serves to preempt more threatening forms or degrees of antistatist violence. Fortunately, the quality of Lochte's reasoning—which, if adopted as policy, might have had the effect of reducing the potential for armed struggle to little more than that of the "revolutionary theater" already evident in the nonviolent movements of most liberal democracies—eluded the bulk of his rather duller counterparts; see generally Peter J. Katzenstein, *West Germany's Internal Security Policy: State and Violence in the 1970s and 1980s* (Ithaca, NY: Center for Studies in International Affairs, Cornell University, 1990). With respect to the idea of militant political staging, in this case within what became the reformist wing of the Black Panther Party, see Robert Burstein, *Revolution As Theater: Notes on the New Radical Style* (New York: Liveright, 1971).

96   For the extraordinarily puerile—and hugely popular—source of the phrase in quotes, see Thomas Harris, *I'm OK, You're OK: A Practical Guide to Transactional Analysis* (New York: Harper & Row, 1969).

97   This notion of prefiguration is featured as a prominent aspect of much past and current pacifist theory; see, e.g., Sharp, *Social Power and Political Freedom* and Epstein, *Political Protest and Cultural Revolution*.

98   This does not have to be so. As Marcuse, following Gramsci, suggested, "methodological disengagement" from the socioeconomic relations prescribed by the status quo can serve a crucial function within the context of revolutionary struggle. But saying this is to say something rather different than that they can supplant such

struggle. See Herbert Marcuse, *An Essay on Liberation* (Boston: Beacon Press, 1971) p. 6. For development of the premise under the rubric of "prefigurative relations," see Carl Boggs, "Marxism, Prefigurative Communism, and the Problem of Workers' Control," *Radical America*, Vol. 11, No. 6 (November 1977) p. 100. On the Gramscian backdrop, see Boggs's *The Two Revolutions: Gramsci and the Dilemmas of Western Marxism* (Boston: South End Press, 1984), especially pp. xi, 107–8, 114n48, and 289–91. For attempts to apply the concept in a rather flawed manner, see Abbie Hoffman, *Woodstock Nation* (New York: Vintage Books, 1969) and Jerry Rubin, *We Are Everywhere* (New York: Harper & Row, 1971) For a good summary of Gramsci's thinking on the matter, see Carl Boggs, *The Two Revolutions: Gramsci and the Dilemmas of Western Marxism* (Boston: South End Press, 1984), especially pp. 289–91. Also see Walter L. Adamson, *Hegemony and Revolution: A Study of Antonio Gramsci's Political and Cultural Theory* (Berkeley: University of California Press, 1980), especially pp. 207–22.

99   The psychosocial and political bases for this were well articulated by the early 1970s. See, e.g., Eldridge Cleaver, *Soul on Ice* (San Francisco/New York: Ramparts/McGraw-Hill, 1968) and *Post-Prison Writings and Speeches* (San Francisco/New York: Ramparts/Random House, 1969); George Jackson, *Soledad Brother: The Prison Letters of George Jackson* (New York: Coward-McCann, 1970) and *Blood in My Eye* (New York: Random House, 1972). The conditions generating such sentiments have not changed much since then. See Alphonso Pinkney, *The Myth of Black Progress* (Cambridge: Cambridge University Press, 1984); Manning Marable, *Race, Reform, and Rebellion: The Second Reconstruction in Black America, 1945–1990* (Jackson: University of Mississippi Press, [2nd ed., rev.] 1991).

100 The relationship is not unlike that described by Angela Davis, bell hooks, and others as existing between women of color and white feminism. See Angela Y. Davis, *Women, Race and Class* (New York: Random House, 1981); bell hooks, *Ain't I A Woman: Black Women and Feminism* (Boston: South End Press, 1981) and *Yearning: Race, Gender and Cultural Politics* (Boston: South End Press, 1990); and Elena Featherston, ed., *Skin Deep: Women Writing on Color, Culture and Identity* (Freedom, CA: Crossing Press, 1994).

101 Words are being put in no one's mouth here. Anyone doubting American pacifism's pretensions to status as a revolutionary (rather than reformist) doctrine should see David Dellinger, *Revolutionary Nonviolence* (Indianapolis: Bobbs-Merrill, 1971). If a straw man is set up by use of such terms, pacifists themselves constructed it.

102 See Jacques Ellul, *Propaganda: The Formation of Men's Attitudes* (New York: Alfred A. Knopf, 1965).

103 See, e.g., Dellinger, *Vietnam Revisited*.

104 See Paul Joseph, *Cracks in the Empire: State Politics in the Vietnam War* (Boston: South End Press, 1981) pp. 245–86.

105 Maclear, *Ten Thousand Day War*, p. 200.

106 One of the more interesting takes on this is offered by Norman Mailer in his *Miami and the Siege of Chicago: An Informal History of the Republican and Democratic Conventions of 1968* (New York: Primus, 1968).

107 See Maclear, *Ten Thousand Day War*, pp. 229–30.

108 See Richard Boyle, *Flower of the Dragon: The Breakdown of the U.S. Army in Vietnam* (San Francisco: Ramparts Press, 1972); David Cortright, *Soldiers in Revolt: The American Military Today* (New York: Anchor Books, 1975); Cincinnatus (Lt. Col. Cecil B. Currey), *Self-Destruction: The Breakdown and Decay of the United States Army During the Vietnam Era* (New York: W. W. Norton, 1981).

109 It is an interesting commentary on the depth of American liberal racism that after the killings of literally hundreds of Afroamerican activists by police and military personnel—including quite a number of black college students—responsible establishment types were finally upset when four white kids were gunned down by the National Guard on a Middle American campus. See, as a prime example, James A. Michener, *Kent State: What Happened and Why* (New York: Random House/Reader's Digest, 1971).

110 Mine is a *very* charitable interpretation of the timing. Others have argued that the mass antiwar movement "dissipated in 1971," in conjunction with Nixon's implementing a lottery system of conscription to fill sharply reduced draft levies, rather than when he suspended it altogether in January 1973. See Terry H. Anderson, *The Movement and the Sixties: Protest in America from Greensboro to Wounded Knee* (New York: Oxford University Press, 1995) pp. 380–81.

111 In some ways, the weight of this policy shift fell even harder on Cambodia. See William Shawcross, *Sideshow: Kissinger, Nixon and the Destruction of Cambodia* (New York: Simon and Schuster, 1979).

112 See Tiziano Terzani, *Giai Thong! The Fall and Liberation of Saigon* (New York: St. Martin's Press, 1976); Văn Tiến Dũng, *Our Great Spring Victory* (London: Monthly Review Press, 1977); Wilfred Burchett, *Grasshoppers and Elephants: Why Vietnam Fell* (New York: Urizen, 1977).

113 As the marxist intellectual Isaac Deutscher put it to David Dellinger, A.J. Muste, and Hans Koningsberger in a 1966 discussion of strategy and tactics, "One might say there is an inconsistency in your attitude, a contradiction in your preaching nonviolence and yet accepting morally . . . the violence applied by the Vietcong in Vietnam and probably by the FLN in Algeria." Excerpts from the conversation later appeared under the title "Marxism and Non-Violence" in

Liberation (July 1969) and collected in Deutscher's *Marxism in Our Time* (Berkeley: Ramparts Press, 1971) pp. 79–91.

114 See Dellinger, *Revolutionary Nonviolence*; Sharp, *The Dynamics of Nonviolent Action* (Volume 3 of *The Politics of Nonviolent Action*); Staughton Lynd, ed., *Nonviolence in America: A Documentary History* (Indianapolis: Bobbs-Merrill, 1966); Richard Gregg, *The Power of Non-Violence* (New York: Schocken Books, 1966).

115 Dating accrues from the point of the initial publication of Lenin's *Imperialism: The Highest Stage of Capitalism*. Widely read at the time, the pamphlet has seen continuous reprinting/distribution ever since.

116 There is by now a vast literature on the subject, either positing the thesis directly or strongly implying it. The work of Harry Magdoff, Andre Gunder Frank, Immanuel Wallerstein, Richard Barnett, Eduardo Galeano, and Régis Debray (to list only six prominent examples) falls within this classification, albeit on the basis of a wide range of precepts and motivations.

117 E.g., the 1961 Declaration on the Granting of Independence to Colonial Countries and Peoples (UNGA 1514 (XV), 14 December 1960), online at http://www.un.org/en/decolonization/declaration.shtml.

118 A seminal advancement of this view within the United States (new) left of the 1960s is found in Carl Oglesby's "Vietnamese Crucible: An Essay on the Meanings of the Cold War," in Carl Oglesby and Richard Schaull, *Containment and Change: Two Dissenting Views of American Foreign Policy* (New York: Macmillan, 1967) pp. 157–69. The idea was taken in a rather unintended direction by Karen Ashley et al., "You Don't Need a Weatherman to Know Which Way the Wind Blows," *New Left Notes* (June 18, 1969), reprinted in Jacobs, *Weatherman*, pp. 51–90.

119 Two (among very many) elaborations of this view from the Third World itself may be found in Frantz Fanon, *A Dying Colonialism* (New York: Grove Press, 1965) and Võ Nguyên Giáp, *People's War, People's Army* (New York: Praeger, 1962).

120 See Jean-Paul Sartre's "Preface," in Frantz Fanon, *The Wretched of the Earth* (New York: Grove Press, 1966) pp. 7–26.

121 See Michael Carver, *War Since 1945* (New York: G.P. Putnam and Sons, 1981).

122 For a lucid articulation of this principle, see Joseph, *Cracks in the Empire*, especially pp. 43–74. On military doctrines, see Maj. John S. Pustay, *Counterinsurgency Warfare* (New York: Free Press, 1965); Michael T. Klare and Peter Kornbluh, eds., *Low Intensity Warfare: Counterinsurgency, Proinsurgency, and Antiterrorism in the Eighties* (New York: Pantheon Books, 1988).

123 Such a proposition, loosely termed "strangulation theory," was quite broadly discussed within the new left during the period 1967–69

and found perhaps its clearest expression in Bill Ayers, "A Strategy to Win," *New Left Notes* (September 12, 1969), reprinted in Jacobs, *Weatherman*, pp. 183–95. It is quite instructive to note that much of the criticism of the undertakings of Weatherman and similar groups by the left was that their actions were "premature" (see Lerner, "Politics of Despair"). There also seems to have been a particular horror that it was white radicals who were resorting to armed struggle. The whole debate appears to rest, at bottom, on a perverse extension of Maoist principles of revolutionary warfare from the national to the geopolitical realm. See Mao's *On Protracted War* (Peking: Foreign Languages Press, 1977).

124   For applications of the Gramscian concept of internal colonialism to the U.S., see Robert Blauner's "Internal Colonialism and Ghetto Revolt," in his *Racial Oppression in America* (New York: Harper & Row, 1972) pp. 82–110; Mario Barrera, Carlos Muñoz, and Charles Ornelas, "The Barrio as an Internal Colony," *Urban Affairs Annual Review*, Vol. 6 (Beverly Hills, CA: Sage, 1972) pp. 565–98. On positioning for armed struggle, see Abraham Guillen, *Philosophy of the Urban Guerrilla* (New York: William Morrow, 1973) and Carlos Marighella, *Mini-Manual of the Urban Guerrilla* (Boulder, CO: Paladin Press, 1985 reprint of 1969 original).

125   This is a pronounced trend in American leftist thinking. See, e.g., Steve Rosskamm Shalom, ed., *Socialist Visions* (Boston: South End Press, 1983).

126   Exactly why is it that the Third World is supposed to bear the brunt of destroying colonialist power while the "opposition" within the colonizing powers essentially sits by waiting for "the moment?" How this bloody task is to be completed is never quite explained. The question of why it would not be more appropriate for mother country radicals to bloody themselves going after the *source* of the problem while the Third Worlds busy themselves prefiguring the outcome is apparently not considered a polite conversational topic by the American left. See, e.g., Adam Roberts, *Civilian Resistance as a National Defense: Non-Violent Action Against Aggression* (Harrisburg, PA: Stackpole Books, 1968) p. 57.

127   The kind of appropriation involved occurs intellectually as well as materially. For a classic example of the former, see Jerry Mander's *In the Absence of the Sacred: The Failure of Technology and the Survival of the Indian Nations* (San Francisco: Sierra Club Books, 1991).

128   Witness, for instance, the fact that Gene Sharp's "revolutionary" tract, *Social Power and Political Freedom* is introduced by no less than Senator Mark O. Hatfield. Recall as well the example of Moratorium organizer Sam Brown (see note 79).

129 For an early and very sharp framing of the question of white skin
     privilege, see Noel Ignatin and Ted Allen, "White Blindspot (1967)"
     in *Understanding and Fighting White Supremacy: A Collection* (Chicago:
     Sojourner Truth Organization, 1976).

130 As Lucy Dawidowicz puts it on p. 371 of *War Against the Jews*, "Civil
     disobedience as a strategy of political opposition can succeed
     only with a government ruled by conscience." The assumption
     of American pacifism—contra evidence—such as its endorse-
     ment of black chattel slavery, expropriation of the northern half of
     Mexico, Hawai'i, Puerto Rico, and the Philippines, and genocide
     of American Indians and Filipinos during the nineteenth and early
     twentieth centuries—has always been that the U.S. government is
     such an entity. In addition to the works already cited, see Theodore
     Paullin, *Introduction to Non-Violence* (Philadelphia: Pacifist Research
     Bureau, 1944); Gene Sharp, *Exploring Nonviolent Alternatives* (Boston:
     Porter Sargent, 1960); Harvey Seiffert, *Conquest by Suffering: The Process
     and Prospects of Nonviolent Resistance* (Philadelphia: Westminster Press,
     1965); A. Paul Hare and Herbert H. Blumberg, eds., *Nonviolent Direct
     Action: American Cases: Social-Psychological Analyses* (Cleveland: Corpus
     Books, 1968); Clarence Marsh Case, *Non-Violent Coercion: A Study in
     the Methods of Social Pressure* (New York: J.S. Orzer, 1972).

131 The process has hardly been restricted to Germany. For a summary
     of its application in Spain, see Hugh Thomas, *The Spanish Civil War*
     (New York: Harper & Row, 1961), especially pp. 1–116; for Italy,
     see Richard Collier, *Duce! A Biography of Benito Mussolini* (New York:
     Viking Press, 1971), especially pp. 83–133; for the USSR, see Robert
     Conquest, *The Great Terror: Stalin's Purge of the Thirties* (New York:
     Macmillan, 1968). That the United States has already flirted with
     the same process, even at the very height of its power, is amply
     revealed in Victory S. Navasky's *Naming Names* (New York: Viking
     Press, 1980) and David Caute's *The Great Fear: The Anti-Communist
     Purge Under Truman and Eisenhower* (New York: Simon and Schuster,
     1978).

132 It should be recalled that the Jews were not the only, or even the first,
     "enemies of the state" targeted by the nazis. Dachau and similar
     concentration camps were originally opened in the mid-1930s to
     house communists, socialists, social democrats, key trade union-
     ists, pacifists, and homosexuals. See Höhne, *Order of the Death's Head*,
     pp. 145–214; Krausnick et al., *Anatomy of the SS State*, pp. 199–204.

133 Bettelheim, foreword to Nyiszli, *Auschwitz*, p. x. On the "it can't
     happen here" syndrome, see Bud Schultz and Ruth Schultz, *It Did
     Happen Here: Recollections of Political Repression in America* (Berkeley:
     University of California Press, 1989).

134   Bettelheim, foreword to Nyiszli, *Auschwitz*, p. xi.

135   See, e.g., Erik H. Erikson and Huey P. Newton, *In Search of Common Ground* (New York: W. W. Norton, 1973).

136   This outcome runs exactly counter to the rationalist expectations so optimistically posited by Jürgen Habermas in his *Knowledge and Human Interests* (Boston: Beacon Press, 1971). It comes much closer to the sort of irrationality disguised as rational opinion described by Russell Jacoby in *Social Amnesia: A Critique of Conformist Psychology from Adler to Laing* (Boston: Beacon Press, 1976).

137   This leaves aside the Eastern traditions of Hindu and Buddhist pacifism, which in certain variants fuse theology and politics in the manner described; see, e.g., Adam Roberts, "Buddhism and Politics in South Vietnam," *The World Today*, Vol. 21, No. 6 (June 1965) pp. 240–50. In the West, we also find subsets which fit this pattern; see, e.g., Margaret E. Hirst, *The Quakers in Peace and War* (New York: George H. Doran, 1923). Usually, however, we find a much shallower, less consistent and more opportunistic expression of such thinking in the U.S. See, e.g., William Robert Miller, *Nonviolence: A Christian Interpretation* (New York: Association Press, 1964).

138   See, e.g., Wilhelm Reich's *The Mass Psychology of Fascism* (New York: Farrar, Straus and Giroux, 1971). On the other side of the ideological coin, see Richard Crossman, ed., *The God That Failed* (London: Hamish Hamilton, 1950).

139   A viewing of *Triumph of the Will*, Leni Riefenstahl's celebrated film on the Nuremburg rallies, conveys the idea quite well.

140   See Eric Hoffer, *The True Believer* (New York: Harper & Row, 1951). Also see Reich, *Mass Psychology of Fascism*. At another level, see Max Weber, *The Protestant Ethic and the Spirit of Capitalism* (New York: Charles Scribner's Sons, 1958).

141   See Steven Jay Gould, "Taxonomy as Politics: The Harm of False Classification," *Dissent* (Winter 1990) pp. 73–78.

142   The point can be illustrated anecdotally almost infinitely. For just one example, there is a matter which occurred at the 1982 Midwest Radical Therapy Conference near Boone, Iowa. Here, a noted "pacifist feminist," who quite consistently and vocally prided herself on never having lifted a finger in physical opposition to such state policies as oppression of the domestic black community or genocide in Southeast Asia, and who was quite arrogant in her superior disassociation from those who did not share her "correct" vision of political appropriateness in this regard, proceeded to physically assault a black man who failed to extinguish his cigarette when she instructed him to do so. Similar examples are legion.

143 See Joel Kovel, *White Racism: A Psychohistory* (New York: Pantheon Books, 1970).

144 John Tomlinson, *Cultural Imperialism* (Baltimore: Johns Hopkins University Press, 1991). The process works as well in reverse as it does when projected into the future. See Robert Young, *White Mythologies: Writing History and the West* (London/New York: Routledge, 1990).

145 This premise is underscored, perhaps unintentionally, in Donald L. Nathanson's *Shame and Pride: Affect, Sex, and the Birth of the Self* (New York: W. W. Norton, 1992).

146 With only a minor reinterpretation, this point becomes an essential subtext of both Reich and Marcuse. See Paul A. Robinson, *The Freudian Left: Wilhelm Reich, Geza Roheim, Herbert Marcuse* (New York: Harper & Row, 1969).

147 See Hilberg, *Destruction of the European Jews* (1961 ed.) pp. 219–23.

148 For example, *The Compact Edition of the Oxford English Dictionary* (1971 ed.) defines praxis as "doing, acting, action, practice."

149 See Lawrence S. Stepelevich, "August von Cieszkowski: From Theory to Praxis," *History and Theory*, Vol. 13, No. 1 (Winter 1974) pp. 39–52. The quotation actually derives from Cieszkowski's *Prolegomena zur Historiosophie*, published in Berlin, 1838.

150 Karl Marx, "Theses on Feuerbach," in T.B. Bottomore and Maximilien Rubel, eds., *Karl Marx: Selected Writings in Sociology and Social Philosophy* (New York: Penguin Books, 1967) p. 83.

151 Karl Marx, *The Poverty of Philosophy* (New York: International, 1969) p. 173.

152 G.W.F. Hegel, *The Philosophy of History* (New York: Dover, 1956) p. 33.

153 Richard Kilminster, *Praxis and Method: A Sociological Dialogue with Lukács, Gramsci and the Early Frankfurt School* (London: Routledge & Kegan Paul, 1979) pp. 264–65.

154 This sentiment goes, of course, to Marx's famous pronouncement in his "Theses on Feuerbach" that the object of theory is not to understand history but to change it, later recast by Lenin as the dictum that "without revolutionary theory there can be no revolutionary practice."

155 This is as opposed to the continuing elaboration of and increasingly esoteric preoccupation with "grand theory": critical theory in the manner of Herbert Marcuse and Jürgen Habermas (as well as the "Adorno revival"), semiotic theory in the manner of Umberto Eco and Jean Baudrillard, structuralist theory in the manner of Louis Althusser, and so on. It is also as opposed to journalistic sorts of endeavors recounting the concrete aspects of various liberatory struggles without attempting to extrapolate formal tenets of tactical praxis for application elsewhere.

156   As Deutscher observed in "Marxism and Non-Violence": "It is said that Marxism suits the underdeveloped countries but not the advanced and industrial west." In effect, Marx is stood squarely on his head insofar as he was clear that his notion of revolution could only occur in the most advanced countries.

157   Leon Trotsky, *The History of the Russian Revolution* (New York: Pathfinder, 1971); Jerome Ch'en, *Mao and the Chinese Revolution* (London: Oxford University Press, 1967); Che Guevara, *Guerrilla Warfare* (New York: Monthly Review, 1961); Henri Weber, *Nicaragua: The Sandinista Revolution* (London: Verso, 1981); David Martin and Phyllis Johnson, *The Struggle for Zimbabwe* (New York: Monthly Review Press, 1981).

158   See Ernest Harsh and Tony Thomas, *Angola: The Hidden History of Washington's War* (New York: Pathfinder, 1976); Gérard Chaliand, *Armed Struggle in Africa: With the Guerrillas in "Portuguese" Guinea* (New York: Monthly Review Press, 1969); Richard Leonard, *South Africa at War: White Power and Crisis in Southern Africa* (Westport, CT: Lawrence Hill, 1983); John Ya-Otto, *Battlefront Namibia* (Westport, CT: Lawrence Hill, 1981); Maria Esther Gilio, *The Tupamaro Guerrillas: The Structure and Strategy of the Urban Guerrilla Movement* (New York: Saturday Review Press, 1970). For the most topical survey of the Western Hemisphere, see Liza Gross, *Handbook of Leftist Guerrilla Groups in Latin America and the Caribbean* (Boulder, CO: Westview Press, 1995).

159   Concerning Fanon's theoretics in this regard, see B. Marie Perinbam, *Holy Violence: The Revolutionary Thought of Frantz Fanon* (Washington, DC: Three Continents Press, 1982). Also see Irene L. Gendzier, *Frantz Fanon: A Critical Study* (New York: Vantage Books, 1974), especially "The Question of Violence" (pp. 195–205). On Guevara, see his *Guerrilla Warfare* and Michael Löwy, *The Marxism of Che Guevara: Philosophy, Economics, Revolutionary Warfare* (New York: Monthly Review Press, 1973), especially "Part III: Guerrilla Warfare" (pp. 75–112). On Mao, see his *On Protracted War* (Peking: Foreign Languages Press, 1967) and Stanley Karnow's *Mao and China: From Revolution to Revolution* (New York: Viking, 1972), especially Chapter 12, "Out of the Barrel of a Gun" (pp. 276–96). On Giáp, see his *People's War, People's Army* (New York: Praeger, 1962).

160   Blase Bonpane, *Guerrillas for Peace: Liberation Theology and the Central American Revolution* (Boston: South End Press, 1985) p. 1.

161   Ibid., p. 8.

162   Significant portions of the Italian left have renounced nonviolence as a strategy or method altogether. See Alessandro Silj, *Never Again Without a Rifle: The Origins of Italian Terrorism* (New York: Karz, 1979).

163   It is instructive that practitioners of armed struggle from the Third World context are also quite vociferously condemned when they

are audacious enough to carry violence into the very industrialized nations objectively responsible for their colonization. The clearest examples here are the extreme equivocation with which the Palestine Liberation Organization is treated by most of the left within late capitalist societies and the outright revulsion visited by progressives upon Muammar Qaddafi concerning his practice of exporting violence back to the societies with the clearest record(s) of engendering it. The same principle applies, of course, to colonized First World nationalities, such as the Irish, Basques, and Québécois, when their military/political organizations—e.g., the IRA—practice the same sort of "turn around" tactics. This all corroborates the notion that the "mother country opposition" considers it a "right" to be exempted from direct violence in any form. On the movements mentioned, see Assata Shakur, *Assata: An Autobiography* (Westport, CT: Lawrence Hill, 1987); Ronald Fernandez, *Los Macheteros: The Wells Fargo Robbery and the Violent Struggle for Puerto Rican Independence* (New York: Prentice Hall, 1987); Peter Matthiessen, *In the Spirit of Crazy Horse* (New York: Viking Press, [2nd ed.] 1991); Tim Pat Coogan, *The IRA: A History* (New York: Roberts Rinehart, 1993); Robert P. Clark, *Negotiating with ETA: Obstacles to Peace in Basque Country, 1975–1988* (Reno: University of Nevada Press, 1990); and Tom Vague, *Televisionaries: The Red Army Faction Story, 1963–1993* (San Francisco: AK Press, 1994).

164 See Tony Geraghty's *Who Dares Wins: The Story of the Special Air Service, 1950–1980* (London: Arms and Armor Press, 1980) and *Inside the SAS* (London: Arms and Armor Press, 1987).

165 See Robert Taber, *War of the Flea: How Guerrilla Fighters Could Win the World* (New York: Citadel Press, 1970).

166 For an interesting examination of "terrorist" thinking and methods, as well as adequate reconstruction of its application between 1970 and 1995—albeit within a rather reactionary ideological framework—see Roberta Goren, *The Soviet Union and Terrorism* (London/Boston: George Allen & Unwin, 1984). Ideological balance can be obtained through Edward S. Herman's *The Real Terror Network: Terrorism in Fact and Propaganda* (Boston: South End Press, 1984).

167 The ineffectuality of the U.S. and other neocolonialist powers in attempting to offset the proliferation of guerrilla wars since 1950, creating "counterinsurgency" doctrine and units, is evident in a number of studies. A sampling would include Donald Duncan, *The New Legions* (New York: Random House, 1967); Lt. Col. Anthony B. Herbert, with James T. Wooten, *Soldier* (New York: Holt, Reinhart and Winston, 1973); Col. Charlie A. Beckwith with Donald Knox, *Delta Force: A Memoir by the Founder of the U.S. Military's Most Secretive Special-Operations Unit* (New York: Harcourt, 1983).

168   Louis Althusser, *For Marx* (New York: Vintage Books, 1970) p. 251.

169   Ernest Gellner, "Foreword," in J.G. Merquior, *The Veil and the Mask: Essays on Culture and Ideology* (London: Routledge & Kegan Paul, 1979) p. 2.

170   Merquior, *The Veil and the Mask*, p. 29.

171   Those confused about the distinction inhering between reform and revolution might wish to consult John and Barbara Ehrenreich's "From Resistance to Revolution," *Monthly Review*, Vol. 19, No. 11 (April 1968). Another useful perspective can be found in the section titled "Rebellion and Revolution," in George Katsiaficas, *The Imagination of the New Left: A Global Analysis of 1968* (Boston: South End Press, 1987) pp. 179–86.

172   Kwame Ture (Stokely Carmichael), speech at the Auraria Campus Student Center, Denver, Colorado, November 24, 1985.

173   Put another way, it is simply to gain a different sort of appreciation of Carl von Clausewitz's famous dictum that war is merely politics pursued by other means. Conversely, politics would be war pursued in the same manner.

174   See Nicos Poulantzas, *Fascism and Dictatorship: The Third International and the Problem of Fascism* (London: Verso, 1979), especially "Forms of the Ideological Crisis: The Crisis of Revolutionary Organizations" (pp. 143–46). Such outcomes are posited, however unintendedly, in Bertram Gross, *Friendly Fascism: The Face of Power in America* (Boston: South End Press, 1982).

175   The term is employed within its precise rather than its popularized meaning, i.e., from the Greek *radic*, meaning "source" or "root." The radical therapist is one who pursues problems to their root or source.

176   This requirement may well lead to the application of a variation of the principle posited by Frank Black Elk in his "Observations on Marxism and the Lakota Tradition," in Ward Churchill, ed., *Marxism and Native Americans* (Boston: South End Press, 1983) pp. 137–56. People who are not typically considered as therapists—and who may well not even perceive themselves as such—will be needed to provide therapy to many self-proclaimed radical therapists before the latter can hope to extend assistance to others.

177   A quick sample of some of the best: Kurt Saxon, *The Poor Man's James Bond* (Eureka, CA: Atlan Formularies, 1975); Lt. Col. Anthony B. Herbert, *The Soldier's Handbook* (Englewood, CA: Cloverleaf Books, 1979); W[illiam] E[wart] Fairburn, *Scientific Self-Defense* (San Francisco: Interservice, 1982 reprint of 1931 original); Tony Lesce and Jo-Anne Lesce, *Checklist for Survival* (Cornville, AZ: Desert Publications, 1980). Copy machines are, of course, a handy aid in furthering dissemination—and to avert putting undue revenue into the hands of the

right. This is not to mention the incredible range of official military training and field manuals (e.g., *Ranger Training Manual*; *Special Forces Handbook*; *Booby Traps, Escape and Evasion*; *Explosives and Demolitions*; and *Your M-16 Rifle*) available by law at essentially no charge through the U.S. Government Printing Office in Washington, DC.

178 This is to reiterate Che Guevara's contention, "at the risk of sounding ridiculous," that "the true revolutionary is guided by a sense of love" (i.e., "to love, one must fight"). See Michael Löwy, *The Marxism of Che Guevara*, p. 54. Or, to return to Deutscher's "Marxism and Non-Violence": "There is a whole dialectic of violence and nonviolence implied in the Marxist doctrine from its beginnings. . . . As Marxists, we have always preached . . . the need to overthrow capitalism by force [yet retain] the aspiration to transform societies in such a way that violence should cease forever as the necessary and permanent element in the regulation of the relationship between society and individuals, between individuals and individuals. In embracing the vision of a nonviolent society, Marxism . . . has gone further and deeper than any pacifist preachers of nonviolence have ever done. Why? Because Marxism has laid bare the roots of violence in our society, which the others have not done. Marxism has set out to attack those roots; to uproot violence not just from human thoughts, not just from human emotions, but to uproot [it] from the very bases of the material existence of society." Although strongly anti-marxist in my political perspectives and practice, I must admit that on these points I wholeheartedly concur with the views expressed.

A Debate Revisited

by Michael Ryan

I wrote my essay in this book as the basis for a speech i intended to give at an "Alliance for Non-Violent Action" gathering at a religious retreat at Lake Scugog in the southern Ontario countryside some thirty years ago. At the time, it would not have occurred to me that it would someday be going into a third edition in a radically different world, one in which i was no longer a young activist but was, in fact, a forgotten activist from two or three waves of revolt back.

As i reread this book—the 2007 edition—for the first time since, well, 2007—i was reminded of something my friend Bill always says: "The future holds promise." In my case, that would be the promise of better thinking and less turgid prose. So, rereading this was a bit of a trip down memory lane for me. I realize that many of the people who will read this third edition may not have been born when it was written, or if they had been were very young. Much of what has happened in the past twenty-eight years, triggered by the fall of the Berlin Wall, the precipitous collapse of the Soviet Union thereafter, and the rise of an increasingly unipolar world and the security state, has served to make this little book a period piece.

Where once we had Third World national liberation organizations and armies, now we have Al-Qaeda, ISIS, and other islamofascists. Where once we had guerrilla groups assassinating politicians, diplomats, CIA agents, and corporate barons, now we have disaffected young Muslims stabbing foot soldiers and mowing down asshole cartoonists. Where once we had native peoples, blacks, Puerto Ricans, and Mexicanos calling for the dismemberment of the North American settler empire, now we have discussions of how we will create "inclusion."

So, what's my point? The world in which *Pacifism as Pathology* was written is so far removed from the world i now live in that i sometimes remember it like somebody had a dream and told me about it—which makes this book going into a third edition at this juncture an issue worth considering.

My dear friend Karl, who owns a cool little book company called Kersplebedeb, which publishes, among other things, a fair number of books by the very much existing political prisoners from the no longer existing organizations that still offered a focal point when i originally wrote my essay, tells me that small books are cheap, so they sell well. (My second-grade teacher would certainly have written "run-on sentence" in the margin for that one, but I'm too lazy to fix it up.) I like to flatter myself that there are other reasons.

One thing i think when flattering myself, for example, is that when you excise what is at this point archaic, you are still left with a very real set of issues that must be addressed if we are to place revolution on the agenda again, because when we talk about revolution, we are talking about (here i borrow my friend Scott's list): vision, goals, strategies, and tactics.[1]

First, "vision": not to be confused with hallucination—i.e., the vision must be dialectical in nature; it must take into consideration what is possible given the existing social/productive system (they are so tightly intertwined at this point as to constitute a singular system, in my never-terribly-humble opinion). We've got to be able to get there from here—we need a realistic roadmap. That said, i can't help but agree with Slavoj Žižek when he says, "The only realist option is to do what appears impossible within this system. This is how the impossible becomes possible."[2] Or, put another way: start out asking for quite a bit more than you think you can ever get or you'll just keep backsliding. I'm not about to hazard a vision of the best of all possible future worlds here—that would be stupid and arrogant, and i try to keep my arrogance intellectually defensible.

Goals: yep, need a few of those on the way to paradise—i would suggest the following as starting points:

An end to genocidal war in the Third World or global South or whatever you wanna call it—I mean Europeans (within which i include their descendants in the Americas, Australia, New Zealand, and anywhere else i might have forgotten) killing and enslaving everyone else and stealing their shit. An end to destroying the earth to pop your toaster, fuel your car, and like that—I mean, do you really need to drive fast to the apocalypse eating warm toast? It would also probably be a good idea to stop persecuting people because of their race or religious beliefs or gender or gender identification or what they wear or don't wear. . . . Of course, everything possible, nonviolent or otherwise, need be done to put an end to the growing use of a militarized apparatus—both public and private—to police poor and marginalized communities. In short, we need to put an end to this Trayvon Martin and Ferguson sort of shit—not only because basic human solidarity demands we do so, and that is reason enough, but because what we are witnessing is the refinement of a surveillance/ security state that has as its first priority closing all avenues to protest and resistance at a time when contradictions are sharpening within the First World. (A quick eye to history will show that marginalized communities and social sectors are always the testing grounds for new repressive techniques and technologies.) Of course, while addressing the increasing paramilitary and counterinsurgency policing, we need to keep in mind the organized right, which maintains a sporadic and deadly armed practice. Yet again, history shows that the overlap between these two demographics will be uncomfortably high.

Small-scale and local initiatives are important, too. Things like protecting urban green spaces (or, let's go crazy, building some more), making public transportation accessible to everyone all the time (i.e., making all those buses and subways accessible to people with mobility issues, and not by 2090 or some fucking thing), stopping government cutbacks, having free and accessible post-secondary education, etc.

Let's not forget though, unless we stop the omnicide, all this good shit is just rearranging the furniture on the *Titanic*. Bottom line: all these things and a whole lot more that could be summed up as genuine freedom and equality and respect for the totality of the universe need to get dealt with post-haste, so no matter how insurmountable it seems, we should probably start now.

Strategy and tactics: first we need to understand that they are two different things; one (tactics) is in the service of the other (strategy). So what precisely do i mean by strategy. Strategy is the approach the movement takes to attacking the state and capital (much more powerful forces) at their weak points (ideological and practical)—in short, the web of theory and practice a dialectical analysis gives rise to. Politics in command, as Mao put it.[3] There are difficult decisions to make about one's relationship to "the masses" in that equation, and, in my opinion, given that most of the population is and will remain for some time to come centrist on a good day for a half an hour, there are times and situations that require one to act even if it bypasses or perhaps even pisses off said masses. All of that and a bunch of other situational details are the factors that allow one to establish a strategy. Any strategy must, of course, be flexible—I would argue that if a "strategy" is inflexible, it is not a strategy—it's a dogma. Flexibility in this context, of course, means flexibility of tactics, as well, or particularly.

As Ed Mead wrote in his preface to the 1998 edition of this book, "The object is to win." In this regard ethics are essential, but ethics, unlike morality, is not a set of rules—"Thou shalt not . . ."—it is individual and flexible. An individual's ethics might circumscribe her or his behavior, but they, de facto, cannot be imposed on another person. What is to be assessed is whether a proposed tactic, be it an electoral campaign, a petition, a letter-writing campaign, a legal challenge, a demonstration, a sit-in or blockade, an act of sabotage, or even guerrilla action, will fruitfully serve the strategy, allowing us to achieve our goals, and thereby helping us to further unfold our vision. I'll tip my hand here; i haven't voted since 1980, and i consider a focus on electoral politics to be worse than reinventing the wheel; it would amount to reinventing the flat tire.

That said, the kind of guerrilla activity i was able to point to when i wrote the original essay back in 1987 is not likely to be a option at this point—without lots and lots and lots of thinking and planning. So, if you're considering that sort of thing, do lots and lots and lots of thinking and planning.

There are two obvious barriers to that sort of activity these days. One is the aforementioned security state, with its ubiquitous surveillance cameras, the tracking of computers and cell phones,[4] and on and on—you get my point. That, however, is only a small problem; the real problem for that particular tactic (not strategy) is, if i may once again quote Mao, that "the guerrilla must move amongst the people as a fish swims in the sea."[5] Our sea done dried up, so we need to deal with the drought before we go swimming. There are some hopeful signs in recent years that things might be beginning to turn around, e.g., the Arab Spring, Occupy, and, in Québec, where i live, the 2012 student movement that became a generalized movement for social equality before running its course. None of these were revolutionary, however; they were essentially movements for bourgeois democratic reforms and inclusion, and that is the case whether they were peacefully occupying and blockading or engaging in low level militant skirmishes with the riot squad (remember that whole strategy vs. tactics thing)—a black leather jacket, a motorcycle helmet, and a rock in your hand doesn't make you a revolutionary; it makes you someone wearing a black leather jacket and motorcycle helmet and carrying a rock. When you throw that rock through a bank window i may well feel a certain *Schadenfreude*, but it is not a de facto revolutionary act, it's largely an insurance issue. Hopefully i am making myself clear: my argument was not and is not that only militant and armed activity can be revolutionary or that it ever automatically is.

However, what i just *did not* say is that revolutionary change can occur without violence—never happened, never will. Nor will you wake up some Thursday morning and discover that militant resistance to the state and capital is required and throw together a plan over breakfast—not even if you're a really slow eater. Anyone who sees their role lying in that sort of militant resistance needs to start doing lots and lots and lots of thinking and planning—particularly about security concerns—like now, with maybe the occasional minor foray into action to test the waters.

However that's all going to sort itself out, the time is far past due for us to develop a vision, set some goals, craft a strategy, and determine the best tactics for achieving our ends. If you think that's a petition or a letter of protest, get writing; if you think that's a court challenge, file the papers; if you think it's a demo, get walking; if you think it's forming a new political party, you're wrong; if you think it's a militant assault on the state and capital, do lots and lots and lots of thinking and planning, then hit the motherfuckers.[6]

When you're sitting around considering all of this, should you decide that you and your three friends have the perfect strategy or tactic, pull you head out of your ass and, to paraphrase Mao, smell a hundred flowers bloom and let a hundred schools of thought contend.[7]

As a final comment, just let me add: we really, really need to get our shit together here, or *we're all going to die!*[8]

On that note, i bid you adieu and wish you all the best in your future endeavors.

Notes

1   I'm told you can say "revolution" again—but if not, what i mean is: a complete social, economic, intellectual, emotional, and "anything you think i forgot" transformation of life on planet earth, such that we have some vague chance of survival and some sense of a starting point for building a world where—to quote Marx—who never really went out of fashion in the academy—wealth will be created and distributed on the basis of "from each according to his ability, to each according to his needs."

2   I realize i should reference this quote, but it's from a list of quotes i jotted down without references. Trust me, he said it, and even if he hadn't i'd still think it, which is all that's important here. Anyway, i haven't got a university job that i can lose because someone doesn't like me but claims my footnotes are the problem, so i can write whatever i want in a footnote with impunity.

3   "Chairman Mao Reviews Mighty Cultural Revolutionary Contingents for the 7th Time," *Peking Review*, Vol. 9, No. 47 (November 18, 1966) pp. 5–7, online at https://www.marxists.org/subject/china/peking-review/1966/PR1966-47b.htm.

4   That handy little GPS tracker we almost all carry around in our pockets and play with incessantly—standing on the street corner waiting for the light, in line waiting for a coffee, at the grocery store, while having dinner with friends, when we wake up in the middle of the night and have nothing better to do—seriously, folks, put that fucking thing away and stop being so bloody rude—it would give you a lot more time to think and plan!

5   Quoted in Scott Nicholas Romaniuk and Stewart Tristan Webb, eds., *Insurgency and Counterinsurgency in Modern War* (Boca Raton, FL: CRC Press, 2015) p. 23.

6   In these heady days of irritatingly diversionary and pointless political correctness, it behooves me stress that I have nothing against either mothers or people who fuck them.

7   All of these Mao references might make you think I am or used to be a Maoist—you would be wrong. The closest I ever got to Maoism was at the wrong end of a two by four, and I think that anyone who believes that Maoism is the solution in the early twenty-first century is guilty of the confusion between vision and hallucination I mentioned above—but hey, dude was no slouch in the brains department. Being a diabolical piece of shit doesn't make you an idiot; if it did, we'd have won by now.

8   We'll probably all be standing around playing with our cell phones when the apocalypse occurs.

On Ward Churchill's "Pacifism as Pathology": Toward a Revolutionary Practice

by Michael Ryan

It is important to explain how i come to be debating Ward Churchill's essay "Pacifism as Pathology." While i endorse as accurate the basic tenets of Churchill's argument, i am not speaking for Ward Churchill; i am only attempting to use Churchill's paper as a starting point for an analysis of where we find ourselves in Canada today.

In Montreal, where i live, i've been involved since 1978 in what is now called civil disobedience, having chalked up five arrests engaging in this rather peculiar behavior. These years of sporadic involvement with nonviolent resistance have left me totally disillusioned with the activity of the peace movement in Canada on virtually every possible level.

Some Definitions

To begin to seriously discuss our common points and our differences, i think it is necessary that we have shared definitions. Much of the debate these days, pro and con pacifism and nonviolence, is, it appears to me, skewed by a near total lack of common language. I therefore offer specific definitions of key terms as i use them.

Regarding pacifism, i accept Churchill's definition of true pacifism: a belief that precludes infliction of violence upon others, but which does not bar the absorption of violence by adherents.[1]

Regarding nonviolence, i use a definition offered by Kelly Booth: "Mutual bending and fitting is the very essence of nonviolence."[2]

And, regarding violence, i again draw upon Booth: "Violence is the imposing of a form, or a set of conditions, on another party without regards to the others' interests, or without sensitivity to their situation."[3]

Arguments for Nonviolence

Arguments for nonviolence seem to fall into two basic categories: ideological and practical. The ideological arguments stress an alleged moral superiority of nonviolence. Essentially, this argument holds that nonviolence is good (right) and violence is bad (wrong). Hence, if we want to be good (in the right), we are morally bound to behave in a nonviolent way.

Along with this basic ideological concept, there is a series of practical arguments against violence used to buttress the moral argument or, in the case of nonviolent activists who are not bound to pacifism, used as arguments against violence in their own right. There are four basic arguments in this category:

1.   There is the ever-popular assertion that the time is not right.
2.   It is contended that violence alienates the people.
3.   It is suggested that violence brings down repression (a kind of practical reworking of the old moral argument that violence begets violence).
4.   Lastly, we are told violence will get us bad press.

To respond to the argument that the time is not right, allow me to turn to an article by Dr. Rosalie Bertell printed in the Cruise Missile Conversion Project's 1984 pamphlet, *A Case for Non-Violent Resistance*. In "Early War Crimes of World War III," Dr. Bertell estimates that if one begins counting with the Hiroshima and Nagasaki bombings, there have already been more than twenty million victims of what she calls the early stages of World War III. She adds:

The prognosis for the world, given this self-destructive and earth-destructive behavior, is poor. As nuclear powers increase their own pollution because of distorted military short-term thinking, the people of their nations will give birth to more physically damaged offspring. These offspring will be less able to cope with the increasingly hazardous environment. Thus a death process is underway, even if there is no catastrophic accident or nuclear holocaust. Just like individual reactions to personal death, so society reacts to species death with the typical stages of denial, anger, barter and finally, it is hoped, realism. For those who have reached the fourth stage there is no pretense that "things are normal" or "one must believe the experts." The stance is to attempt to heal the possibly mortal wounds, or to sit with the dying earth. Honesty is the fundamental medicinal approach.[4]

Given this reality, i am prompted to ask how bad conditions must become before we recognize that the time is right for any and all forms of resistance that can be effectual in putting an end to this madness, before it puts an end to us.

Turning now to the argument that violence alienates the people, i find myself face to face with several undeniable flaws of logic. If violence alienates the people, are we to refrain from engaging in any but passive acts of protest (and here i use the term protest rather than resistance quite consciously) because this will win popular support? If this is the case, i am forced to ask why, after years of consistent non-violent protest, no qualitative growth, and only the slightest quantitative, has occurred within our movement? From these questions, i would go on to suggest that catering our activity to our perception (which might not even be accurate) of the level of resistance acceptable to people, far from being revolutionary, is in fact counter to the development of revolutionary consciousness:

> A party [or, in our case, an organization or movement]
> which *bases itself* on an *existing* average level of con-
> sciousness and activity, will end up *reducing* the present
> level of both. It is the party's responsibility to *lead*, to
> *change* the existing level of consciousness and activity,
> raise them to higher levels. (emphasis in original)[5]

It is clear that the peace movement, rather than offering vital connections and a direction for popular discontent (which plainly exists), has failed to offer anything more than a repetitive and increasingly boring spectacle. The government in Ottawa—and the general populous—has increasingly taken to yawning at our activities.

The argument that violence brings repression down on the left indicates a naiveté bordering on sheer madness. Do we *really* believe that if we could devise a nonviolent means of eliminating the state we would be allowed to proceed unhindered in carrying it out? The state is violent in its very nature. The police, the army, and prisons stand as immediate, tangible evidence of this. The genocide of Third and Fourth World peoples stands as evidence of this. Canada's role as an arms producer and supplier for the Indonesian colonization of East Timor is a daily, ongoing act of violence. Violence, overt and covert, aggressive and preventive, is fundamental to the function of the Canadian state. No violence issuing from the movement could hope to be more than a pale reflection of the constant violence of the repressive apparatus.

That this violence generally remains invisible is more a statement of our failure than of our success, a reflection of the degree to which we have remained within the limits acceptable to the state. As Mao said in 1939:

> I hold that it is bad as far as we are concerned if a
> person, a political party, an army or a school is not
> attacked by the enemy, for in that case it would defi-
> nitely mean that we have sunk to the level of the enemy.

> It is good if we are attacked by the enemy, since it proves that we have drawn a clear line of demarcation between the enemy and ourselves. It is still better if the enemy attacks us wildly and paints us as utterly black and without a single virtue; it demonstrates that we have not only drawn a clear line of demarcation between the enemy and ourselves but achieved a great deal in our work.[6]

Finally, and intimately connected to the idea that violence creates state repression, is the equally curious concept that violence gets the movement bad press (presumably reinforcing the alienation of the people). One wonders how it could be believed that any kind of consistent good press can be expected from media owned by the same corporate interests we are attacking.

To turn to the ideological, or moral, argument favoring nonviolence, an argument i personally believe to be more worthy of respect than the tactical argument(s), let's examine our relationship to the international struggle and to other peoples struggling for freedom within the borders of North America. When nonviolence is proposed as the only acceptable form of resistance by white militants in North American, it is not, for me, a statement of moral depth but a statement regarding the depth of our white skin privilege.

Our situation as white radicals, and this is especially true for white men, is that of people who, for one reason or another, have chosen to partially break from the oppressor nation we are part of. The conscious choice to break with our culture does not de facto remove the privilege of our position. The very existence of a choice between resistance and acceptance—the fact that all white resisters can ultimately return to the fold—colors our perceptions of both ourselves and of resistance from the outset. The simple choice to resist does not change our perception, if, in fact, it can ever be changed, or remove our white skin privilege.

In the pamphlet *Pornography, Rape, War: Making the Links*, coproduced in 1984 by the Women's Action for Peace and the Alliance for Non-Violent Action, this privilege is explicitly recognized, but in a way that reinforces it:

> As part of a white, middle-class society, we are privileged with some degree of basic humyn rights, respect for humyn dignity, and the possibility of making effective changes through nonviolent means.[7] This, apparently, leads to three responsibilities: First it is our responsibility not to escalate the extent of the use of violence; secondly, it is our responsibility to respond in such a way that recognizes the original fact—that no peoples would choose a violent struggle unless they deemed it necessary for their survival—and our specific privileged capacity to effect change through nonviolent means; thirdly, it is both our capacity and our responsibility to develop and extend the credibility of a commitment to nonviolent responses and resolutions to oppressive conditions.[8]

What is here referred to varyingly as the possibility of making effective changes through nonviolent means and our specific privileged capacity to effect change through nonviolent means is, in fact, more accurately a recognition of our capacity to live without change because our privileged position not only makes that possible but relatively comfortable.

Here, i think that the politics of the comfort zone, as Churchill describes them, hold true for what we are experiencing in the Canadian peace movement. Allow me to quote a section:

> The question central to the emergence and maintenance of nonviolence as the oppositional foundation of American activism has been, by and large, not the truly pacifist formulation, "How can we forge a revolutionary politics within which we can avoid inflicting

violence on others?" On the contrary, a more accurate articulation would be, "What sort of politics might I engage in which will both allow me to posture as a progressive *and* allow me to avoid incurring harm to *myself?*" Hence, the trappings of pacifism have been subverted to establish a sort of politics of the comfort zone, not only akin to what Bettelheim termed "the philosophy of business as usual" and devoid of perceived risk to its advocates, but minus any conceivable revolutionary impetus as well. The intended revolutionary content of true pacifist activism—the sort practiced by the Gandhian movement, the Berrigans, and Norman Morrison—is thus isolated and subsumed in the U.S., even among the ranks of self-professing participants. (emphasis in original)[9]

It seems, in short, that the civil disobedience of the white Canadian peace movement, rather than being a revolutionary practice or an honest expression of protest, has become a form of catharsis, a practice that allows us to cleanse our souls of the guilt of our white skin privilege for ourselves and for each other without posing a threat either to the state or ourselves. We create a theater of pseudoresistance in which everyone has their part. We dutifully announce the time, place, and form of our resistance. The police will report for duty at the appointed time and place. We will sit down and refuse to move until X change occurs in government policy. A pseudodiscourse will occur between the police and the protesters. The media will take some photos and possibly prepare a short report. The police will make inevitable arrests. If all goes smoothly (and, if we have our way, it will), the whole spectacle will be over in under an hour, sometimes as quickly as fifteen minutes.

If just the farce of this theater piece were under consideration, i would be content to call it a living tragicomedy, have myself an ironic laugh, and forget it. Unfortunately, one must also consider the underlying message, for it is at this level that our interests and those of the state, sadly enough, coincide. We are attempting to demonstrate the existence of opposition to state policy. Far from wanting to silence this opposition, however, the state can thrive on it if the message is the right one. The message of civil disobedience as it is now practiced is this: there is opposition in society. The state deals with this opposition firmly but gently, *according to the law.* Unlike some countries, *Canada is a democratic society that tolerates opposition.* Therefore, it is unnecessary for anyone to step outside the forms of protest accepted by this society; *it is unnecessary to resist.*

Do we really believe the state allows small groups to engage in openly planned and publicized protest actions because it is somehow powerless in the face of our truth, superior morality, or whatever? Clearly, the state allows us to engage in these actions because they are harmless, or, worse, because they reinforce the popular myth of Canadian democracy.

This degeneration into the politics of the comfort zone has led to several deformations that reinforce the continuation of this cycle of self-serving protest. One such deformation is the increasing tendency for arrest and the presumed incumbent publicity to become ends unto themselves. Within this framework, the number of arrests one has amassed becomes the proof of one's revolutionary commitment and credentials. This process, particularly rampant among men, where civil disobedience becomes a form of nonviolent machismo, is appropriately described by Judy Costello: "I believe in noncooperation and civil disobedience, but in practice I have seen men use these tools as weapons—seeing who can suffer the most, counting up jail records, feeding on the glory of being able to suffer more."[10]

Another deformation, one which serves as a cushion against breaking with comfort zone politics, is the concept that there is no enemy, that we are *all* victims (oppressed and oppressors alike), victims of a state gone out of control. This concept is undoubtedly the result of the fact that nonviolence is often a white movement response to forms of repression that do not directly affect its members, whether this takes the form of support to the Innu, Azanians, the people of Wollaston Lake or Big Mountain, or the East Timorese. It has become increasingly popular to give a nod to concepts of the oneness of it all held by indigenous peoples when searching for a theoretical underpinning to the concept of no enemy. In this vein, it is perhaps instructive to look at what Rolling Thunder, a traditional native spiritual spokesperson, has to say on this subject:

> The idea I've found in some modern people that there's no good or bad, that it's all the same, it's pure nonsense. I know what they are trying to say, but they don't understand it. Where we're at here in life, with all our problems, there's good and there's bad, and they better know it.[11]

As long as we remain passive and ineffective in our resistance, we will, as Ward Churchill states, leave Third and Fourth World peoples in the front line of the very real and very violent struggle between imperialism and liberation while we continue to reap the benefits of a comfort zone created by their oppression. All the pious statements and the cathartic activities we engage in change nothing. Perhaps we must look ourselves squarely in the face and see ourselves as others often see us.

> If it is true that whites want struggles without pain— and we say that it is—then it's because they don't want new life, don't really want a new order. It means they ain't really dissatisfied with the present arrangement of power and property relations.[12]

Having dealt with what i see as the operative comfort zone politics governing the current peace movement politics, i will now turn to the thought of pacifists and nonviolent activists, both historically and currently, to attempt to ascertain the degree to which pacifism absolutely precludes violence.

Allow me first to turn to the thinking of Henry David Thoreau, particularly to his work "On the Duty of Civil Disobedience" (originally entitled "Resistance to Civil Government"). In this work, Thoreau says, "The only obligation I have a right to assume is to do at any time what I think right."[13]

And later:

> In other words, when a sixth of the population of a nation which has undertaken to be the refuge of liberty are slaves, and subjected to military law, I think it is not too soon for honest men to rebel and revolutionize. What makes this duty all the more urgent is the fact that the country so over-run is not our own, but ours is the invading army.[14]

Thoreau would of course condone such rebellions and revolutionizing taking a nonviolent form. But to find another dimension, we have only to look at his text "A Plea for Captain John Brown," the white, antislavery fighter who engaged in armed struggle against the government in opposition to slavery before finally being arrested at Harpers Ferry during an armed raid and subsequently hanged for treason:

> I do not wish to kill or be killed, but I can foresee circumstances in which both of these things would be by me unavoidable. We preserve the so-called peace of community by deeds of petty violence every day. Look at the policeman's billy and handcuffs! Look at the jail! Look at the gallows! Look at the chaplain of the regiment! We are hoping only to live on the outskirts of this provisional arm. So we defend ourselves and our hen-roosts, and maintain slavery. I know that the mass of my countrymen think that the only righteous

use that can be made of Sharps rifles and revolvers is to fight duels with them, when we are insulted by other nations, or to hunt Indians, or shoot fugitive slaves with them, or the like. I think that for once the Sharps rifles and the revolvers were employed in a righteous cause. The tools were in the hands of one who could use them.[15]

And finally "The question is not about the weapon but the spirit in which you use it."[16]

It is equally instructive to look at the thought of Martin Luther King Jr. on this question. In particular, i would like to look at the CBC Massey Lectures which Dr. King gave in 1967. In a lecture entitled *Conscience and the Vietnam War*, Dr. King said, "Every man of humane convictions must decide on the protest that best suits [his] convictions but we must all protest."[17]

Regarding youth and social action, he said:

But across the spectrum of attitudes towards violence that can be found among radicals is there a unifying thread? Whether they read Gandhi or Frantz Fanon, all radicals understand the need for action—direct, self-transforming and structure-transforming action. This may be their most creative, collective insight.[18]

Finally, Dr. King's position becomes unequivocally clear in the following quote from his lecture *Conscience and Social Change*, concerning the riots of 1967:

This bloodlust interpretation ignores the most striking features of the city riots. Violent they certainly were. But the violence, to a startling degree, was focused against property rather than people. There were very few cases of injury to persons, and the vast majority of the rioters were not involved at all in attacking people. . . . From the facts, an unmistakable pattern emerges: a handful of Negroes used gunfire substantially to intimidate, not to kill; and all of the other participants had a different target—property. . . . I am aware that there are many who wince at the distinction between property and persons, who hold both sacrosanct. My views are not so rigid. A life is sacred. Property is intended to serve life, and no matter how much we surround it with rights and respect, it has no personal being. It is part of the earth man walks on; it is not [human].[19]

I present these rather lengthy quotes because i think it is important that when we draw upon historical figures to support our strategy we recognize that their definitions of violence and nonviolence, of the line between nonviolent and violent resistance, were much less rigid than those we are now in the habit of employing. However, we need not look so far back in history or outside the current white peace movement to find evidence of a recognition that nonviolence does not imply the absolute, constant, and permanent absence of force or violence. I could offer quotes ad nauseam to this effect, but i will restrict myself to the following two. First, Doug Man, in an article entitled "The Movement":

One does not become nonviolent by failing to act (or acting too weakly) to prevent the prior violence; one shares responsibility for it. There are only varying degrees of violence in real situations, and the correct revolutionary action will always be the least violent one appropriate to a given set of circumstances.[20]

Second, Pat James, in an article entitled "Physical Resistance to Attack: The Pacifist's Dilemma, the Feminist's Hope":

Common sense as well as nonviolent principle dictates that an aggressive physical response to a threat is the last choice for self-defense. Any physical response by the victim is likely to be perceived as violence by

the attacker, and the defender should use the least
amount of force necessary to stop the attack.[21]

Were we to accept the level of violence defined/accepted as
within the bounds of nonviolence by Man and James, then i
believe we would find that the ideological distance between
so-called nonviolent resisters and supporters of violent
resistance in Canada today would be one of differences in
analysis and chosen tactics at this point in history, rather
than the absolute moral and strategic abyss we often present
it as. I don't believe there is anyone on any side of the debate
proposing more than appropriate violence, more than necessary force. It is simply a matter of determining, at this historical juncture, what is necessary and appropriate to stem the
flood of violence of modern society, recognizing as we do the
ease with which we, as a privileged social group, can fall back
into the comfort zone available to us in this society as a result
of this ongoing violence. If we do not proceed honestly and
critically, we risk creating a situation where the adherence to
nonviolence takes precedence over achieving the goals that
we set for ourselves.

Nonviolence and the Third World

"National liberation, national renaissance, the restoration of nationhood to the people, commonwealth;
whatever may be the formulas introduced, decolonization is always a violent phenomenon."[22]

This quote from Frantz Fanon poses a hard reality. There has
never been an example of nonviolent liberation in the Third
World. The one experiment with nonviolent decolonization
was the electoral victory of Salvador Allende in Chile, and
this one example was smashed by U.S. imperialism with such
ease and brutality as to virtually eliminate the last vestiges of
any illusion that Western imperialism will allow nonviolent
decolonization. One has only to look to Nicaragua to see

the absolute necessity for the developed capacity for violent response in a nation that frees itself from the imperialist bloc.

Again, one need only look to the African National Congress (ANC) and the example of Nelson Mandela to see why Third World revolutionaries must embrace violence. The ANC did not turn to armed struggle until June 1961, following more than a decade of nonviolent resistance. In 1952, 8,500 ANC supporters were arrested for civil disobedience actions against the pass laws, and, as a result, Mandela, among others, was banned. For continuing nonviolent resistance, Mandela was arrested and charged with treason in 1956, not to be acquitted until 1961. The prosecutor in this trial said, "If any serious threat to white rule were to arise, the shooting of 5,000 natives by machine gun would provide quiet for a long time."[23]

This model was applied against peaceful demonstrators in Sharpeville on March 21, leaving sixty-seven dead. On May 31, 1961, a three-day peaceful strike was broken up by massive police and military intervention. Finally, pushed to the limit, the ANC turned to armed struggle, founding its military wing Umkhonto we Sizwe [Spear of the Nation] on June 26, 1961, and beginning a campaign of sabotage in December of the same year. Mandela, as a leading figure in Umkhonto we Sizwe, was arrested in August of 1962. In his 1963 trial on sedition charges, for which he languished in jail for twenty-seven years, Mandela explained the decision to turn to violence as follows:

> Government violence can only do one thing and that is breed counter-violence. We have warned repeatedly that the government, by resorting continually to violence, will breed counter-violence amongst the people, until ultimately, if there is no dawning of sanity on the part of the government, the dispute will finish by being settled in violence and by force.[24]

Our responsibility goes beyond recognizing why colonized peoples are forced to turn to violence, beyond recognizing the right of colonized peoples to use violent forms of struggle. We must also recognize that there is a dialectical relationship between Third World liberation and international struggles of all other types, that the speed and effectiveness of decolonization in the Third World is in part determined by the effectiveness of our resistance in the asshole of the beast. Our solidarity lies, as George Lakey of the Movement for a New Society has said, in actively working to bring an end to colonialism and imperialism by attacking its centers of power.[25] We must make such resistance central and as complete as possible. This resistance, if it is to be effective, obliges us to absorb some of the violence of the international confrontation. If we fail to do so, we fail to meet our responsibility to play a full and equal role in the international revolution. We will be guilty of what Marcel Péju has called "the wish to build up a luxury socialism upon the fruits of imperialist robbery."[26] We will fail to meet the challenge of Third World peoples, defined by Fanon as follows:

> The Third World does not mean to organize a great crusade of hunger against the whole of Europe. What it expects from those who for centuries have kept it in slavery is that they will help to rehabilitate mankind, and help make man victorious everywhere, once and for all. But it is clear that we are not so naive as to think this will come about with the cooperation of European governments. This huge task which consists of reintroducing man into the world, the whole of mankind, will be carried out with the indispensable help of the European people, who must themselves realize that in the past they have often joined the ranks of our common masters where colonial questions were concerned. To achieve this the European peoples must first decide to wake up and shake themselves, use their brains, and stop playing the stupid game of Sleeping Beauty.[27]

We should not be so vain, however, as to believe that if we do not mobilize revolutionary opposition in the center, the international revolution will cease to exist. Rather, we will simply be choosing to remain in the comfort zone while our brothers and sisters in the Third World continue to struggle for international justice at an ever-greater cost to themselves. Meanwhile, we can continue to reap the benefits of their exploitation while rhetorically posing as revolutionaries.

The Internal Colonies

When we talk about colonization of the Third World, national liberation, and so forth, we generally think about South and Central America, Africa, the Middle East, and so on. Seldom do we consider the internal Third and Fourth World colonies within North America. Here, i mean the Native nations, the New Afrikan (black) nation, occupied Puerto Rico, and northern Mexico. I wish now to turn attention to these.

Native Nations

In an article entitled "Radioactive Colonization and the Native American," Ward Churchill and Winona LaDuke demonstrate that native nations exist within both Canada and the United States. These nations, which are victims of neocolonialism, today hold a land base that is about 3 percent of their original. However, the Dine (Navajo) Nation alone has a land base equivalent in size to Luxemburg, Lichtenstein, and Monaco combined, or approximately as large as Belgium, the Netherlands, or Denmark. Further, the Dine Nation alone is richer in natural resources than all six of the abovementioned European nations combined. By these measures, indigenous North American people should, by every standard, be among the wealthiest and healthiest of populations. Instead, by both U.S. and Canadian governmental accounts, they are the very poorest strata of society, experiencing far and away the shortest life expectancies and highest rates of infant mortality, least education, most unemployment, and greatest rates of death by malnutrition, suicide, and exposure. Churchill and LaDuke hold that all this is the direct byproduct of the internal colonization of American Indians, and that the situation must be changed.[28]

They further argue a radical native response—one which they believe is to be found in the program of the American Indian Movement, AIM—is in a position to cripple North American imperialism. This is so because the radical native position (which Churchill has elsewhere termed indigenism) is anti-imperialist both internally and externally. American Indian peoples are in a position to destroy much of the North American imperialist base by challenging its Indian policy and dismembering its domestic territoriality. They can equally cripple U.S. imperialism in its external projection by depriving it of, or at least curtailing its access to, crucial resources, including uranium (about 60 percent of the North American reserves are located within Native American lands) and a range of other critical minerals. The implications for U.S. armaments production, for example, are obvious.[29]

This will not, however, be a peaceful struggle, and we, as Euroamerican radicals inside the North American settler states, must develop a clear position regarding what we will do if this war of genocide that has been going on for some 500 years once again heats up and heads toward a definitive culmination.

New Afrika

The struggle of New Afrikan people for independence is often regarded by the white movement as being almost archetypically violent. A particularly good example of this can be found in the Spring 1987 issue of *Kick It Over* where Malcolm X (El-Hajj Malik El-Shabazz) is described in a footnote as having been a competitor to Martin Luther King Jr., presumably on the basis of Malcolm's belief that the decolonization of black people in America would be a process involving violence.[30] Whites often elect to portray these two men as ideological competitors, a matter reflecting the splits in consciousness of our own movement rather than theirs. In actuality, both Malcolm X and Martin Luther King Jr. shared a single long-term goal—the liberation of black people in America. They could each be found at the same mass actions, and they both ultimately died at the hands of assassins as a result of their lifelong struggles.

We have already looked at what Dr. King had to say regarding violence. A similar look at what Malcolm X had to say on violence reveals that, while there are differences in outlook between the two men, these are not so great as we have been led to believe. In a 1964 speech, Malcolm X said, "Now, I'm not criticizing those here who are nonviolent. I think everyone should do it the way they feel it is best, and I congratulate anyone who can remain nonviolent in the face of all [that confronts us]."[31] In a 1965 interview he goes on:

> I don't favor violence. If we could bring about recognition and respect for our people by peaceful means, well and good. Everybody would like to reach [our] objectives peacefully. But I am also a realist. The only people in this country who are asked to be nonviolent are [the oppressed]. I've never heard anyone go to the Ku Klux Klan and teach them nonviolence, or the [John] Birch Society, or other right-wing elements. Nonviolence is only preached to black Americans and I don't go along with anyone who wants to teach our people nonviolence until someone at the same time is teaching our enemy to be nonviolent. I believe we should protect ourselves by any means necessary when we are attacked by racists.[32]

This position is not unique among supposedly violence-prone black movements. For instance, Point 10 of the *Program of the Black Panther Party* reads:

> We want land, bread, housing, education, clothing, justice, and peace. And our major political objective:

> a United Nations-supervised plebiscite to be held
> throughout the black colony in which only black colo-
> nial subjects will be allowed to participate, for the
> purpose of determining the will of black people as to
> their national identity.[33]

And lest one think the Panthers' policy of armed self-defense
was particularly violent and aggressive, the following quote
from party chairman Bobby Seale's "1969 Instructions to all
Members" is informative:

> No Panther can break the gun law unless his life is
> in danger and the Party recognizes this. If he does,
> we will expel or suspend him depending on the seri-
> ousness of the offense. Panther Party training in this
> area of self-defense includes a study of gun laws, [and]
> safe use of weapons, and there is a strict rule that no
> Party member can use a weapon except in the case of
> an attack on his life—whether the attacker is a police
> officer or any other person. In the case of police har-
> assment the Party will merely print the offending
> officers picture in the newspaper so the officer can be
> identified as an enemy of the people. . . . No attempt
> on his life will be made.[34]

More contemporaneously, Omali Yeshitela, head of the
African People's Socialist Party, has said:

> The question of peace also demands that we use every
> means within our power to arm the African masses
> against the attacks against our people throughout the
> U.S. The question of peace must embrace the idea of
> the self-reliance by the colonized masses to provide
> their own resistance to terror, their own peace.[35]

The theme is clearly repetitive. Wherever we look among the
pronouncements of New Afrikans, it is the same: land, peace,
and self-defense. From the very origin of slavery, through

the COINTELPRO repression—which saw black groups of the 1960s and '70s disrupted, and black leaders imprisoned or liquidated—black people have been the victims of orchestrated genocide. Should we doubt this, we have only to recall the bombing of the MOVE house in Philadelphia on May 13, 1985, and the subsequent blanket exoneration (in May 1988) of all the officials responsible for the mass murder that ensued. It is equally important that we never forget the final announcement of government agents before dropping their bomb: "Attention MOVE! This is America!"

Is it any surprise, given such a history, that nonviolent black organizations, such as the Congress for Racial Equality (CORE) and the Student Nonviolent Coordinating Committee (SNCC), ultimately broke with the constraints of nonviolence? As in the case of American Indians, the struggle of black people demands our concrete support. Black Panther Minister of Defense Huey P. Newton once put it this way:

> When we're attacked and ambushed in the Black Colony, then the white revolutionary students and intellectuals and all other whites who support the Colony should respond by attacking the enemy in their community.[36]

In 1969, Students for a Democratic Society (SDS), one of the main organizations of the North American anti-imperialist movement at that time, recognized the key role of black nationalism in the common struggles against capitalism and imperialism. SDS further noted that "revolutionary nationalism [is] the main factor which ties all the oppressed nations together in their fight against imperialism, and that anything less than complete support on the part of the white left would be a copout on the solidarity which we must give the worldwide movement of the oppressed peoples for liberation".[37]

Puerto Rico

The direct colonization of an island off its coast by the United States and the exploitation of this island for military purposes and as a source of cheap labor and raw materials has led to the rise of a national liberation struggle both on the island itself and in the United States, where many Puertorriqueños have been forced to move because of the artificially depressed economic conditions in their homeland.

Again we have at hand a nonwhite movement within North America forced to confront the question of violence in ways that are qualitatively different from that of whites. The matter need not be belabored, but i will quote from Point 12 of the Young Lords Party Program and Platform, a Puertorriqueño formation similar to the Panthers which was active in the United States until the late 1970s, which states:

> We believe armed self-defense and armed struggle are the only means to liberation. We are opposed to violence—the violence of hungry children, illiterate adults, diseased old people, and the violence of poverty and profit. We have asked, petitioned, gone to courts, demonstrated peacefully, and voted for politicians full of empty promises. But we still ain't free. The time has come to defend the lives of our people against repression and for revolutionary war against the businessman, politician, and police. When a government oppresses our people, we have a right to abolish it and create a new one.[38]

While the Young Lords no longer exist, other independentista organizations have come into being to continue the struggle both on the island of Puerto Rico and inside the United States. Sixteen prominent Puertorriqueño nationalists arrested in an FBI/CIA/military predawn raid on the island in September 1985 were tried in Hartford, Connecticut, on charges related to the actions of the clandestine organization Los Macheteros. As white radicals and revolutionaries supporting such nations as Nicaragua and Third World organizations such as the FMLN, we are duty-bound to also support this Puertorriqueño national liberation struggle that so closely parallels that of other Latin American anticolonial struggles. We cannot allow ourselves to be alienated from it because one of its fronts, which by its very nature requires reliance upon armed actions, lies squarely in the heart of our North American safety zone.

Mexico

Closely related to the Puertorriqueño independentista movement is that for liberation of the northern half of Mexico, the portion north of the Rio Grande expropriated by the United States under the provisions of the 1848 Treaty of Guadalupe Hidalgo. Although the roots of this liberation struggle extend back through history all the way to the U.S. war of conquest which resulted in the treaty, its more recent manifestations began in the mid-1960s with the emergence of Reies Lopez Tijerina's Alianza Federal de Mercedes in New Mexico, Rodolfo "Corky" González's Crusade for Justice in Colorado, and the Brown Berets in California. These were consolidated in the form of the Movimiento Liberación Nacional Mexico (Movement for the National Liberation of Mexico, MLNM), an organization aligned with the Puertorriqueño Fuerzas Armadas de Liberación Nacional (Armed Forces of the National Liberation, FALN). The requirements for anti-imperialist support to this Mexicano independentista movement are essentially the same as with regard to the Puertorriqueño movement (or, for that matter, with regard to Native American and New Afrikan liberation struggles).

Women and Nonviolence

Finally, i would like to look briefly at nonviolence as it applies to women, beginning with two quotes. First:

> As women, nonviolence must begin for us in the refusal to be violated, in the refusal to be victimized. We must find alternatives to submission because our submission—to rape, to assault, to domestic

> servitude, to abuse and victimization of every sort—
> perpetuates violence.[39]

And second:

> The main reason for choosing physical resistance
> to physical attack is that it is most likely to work. . . .
> Researchers report that the more quickly a woman
> responds with physical force, the less likely she will
> be raped, and that early recognition of danger is the
> single most important factor in preventing or deflect-
> ing attack.[40]

When we look at the issue of nonviolent resistance to aggression, we must consider that we are dealing with many separate
experiences. One of the most universal divisions must be violence as it is experienced by women under patriarchy, and violence as it is experienced by men under patriarchy. Clearly, we
recognize the right of women to respond to physical and psychological aggression using whatever means are necessary, up
to and including armed or violent self-defense or retaliation.

Nonviolence: Some Logical Inconsistencies

We accept the necessity of armed struggle in the Third World
because the level of oppression leaves people with no other
reasonable option. We recognize that the actions of Third
World revolutionaries are not aggressive acts of violence but a
last line of defense and the only option for liberation in a situation of totally violent oppression. Similarly, an examination
of the realities confronting American Indians, New Afrikans,
Puertorriqueños, and Mexicanos/Chicanos, should, i believe,
bring us face to face with the fact that the same sorts of Third
and Fourth World circumstances and dynamics exist within
the contemporary borders of the United States and Canada.
Certain sectors of the peace movement have already begun
to recognize this in a rudimentary kind of way. For example,
the following quote comes from an open letter to the peace

movement as a whole by the advisory board of the United Methodist Voluntary Service:

> If real peace is to be achieved, the white peace move-
> ment must aggressively seek leadership and direction
> from blacks, Hispanics, Native Americans, and other
> people of color. They must participate in all aspects of
> organizational planning, decision-making, and out-
> reach. It is only with this active involvement that it will
> be possible to build a truly broadbased, multiracial,
> multicultural movement capable of winning.[41]

I would only add that we must also recognize that the reason such a movement can win is because it has the capacity to meet the violence of the state with a counterviolence of sufficient strength to dismember the heartland of the empire, liberating the oppressed nations within it. Further, we must acknowledge the absolute right of women to respond to the violence of patriarchy with the force necessary to protect themselves. In sum, we must recognize the validity of violence as a necessary step in self-defense and toward liberation when the violence of the system leaves the victim(s) with no other viable option. And it is here the logical inconsistency lies.

We recognize the right of oppressed peoples to respond to their oppression with violence, but we abstain from engaging in violence ourselves. Thus we recognize our own participation in the oppression of other peoples while we also attempt to deny the critical situation in which we ourselves are found today, a circumstance described by Rosalie Bertell in an earlier quote. If, as Bertell suggests, we are sitting upon a dying earth, and consequently dying as a species solely as a result of the nature of our society, if the technology we have developed is indeed depleting the earth, destroying the air and water, wiping out entire species daily, and steadily weakening us to the point of extinction, if phenomena such as Chernobyl are not aberrations, but are (as i insist they are) mere reflections of our daily reality projected at a level where we can at last recognize its true meaning, then is it not time—long past time—when we should do anything, indeed everything, necessary to put an end to such madness? Is it not in fact an act of unadulterated self-defense to do so?

Our adamant refusal to look reality in its face, to step outside our white skin privilege long enough to see that it is killing us not only tangibly reinforces the oppression of people of color the world over, it may well be the single most important contributor to an incipient omnicide, the death of all life as we know it. In this sense, it may well be that our self-imposed inability to act decisively, far from having anything at all to do with the reduction of violence, is instead perpetuating the greatest process of violence in history. It might well be that our moral position is the most mammoth case of moral bankruptcy of all time.

What Is to Be Done?

It is not my purpose here, as i understand it was not Ward Churchill's before me, to suggest that the peace movements in either the United States or Canada adopt a program of armed struggle. Rather, it is my intent, as i assume it was his, to strongly point out that the current strategies of both movements are not revolutionary and can therefore not be expected to lead in positive, or even acceptable, directions for social change. These strategies are nothing but a complex, psychological self-deception that allows us to pose as revolutionaries from within our comfort zones. Churchill's thesis and his analysis are, in my view, 100 percent accurate.

I also find in Churchill's essay the starting point for the process that can reverse the slide into the oblivion of irrelevance—or worse—upon which we currently appear to have embarked. I quote a passage that must be considered key in this regard:

> What is at issue is not . . . the replacement of hegemonic pacifism with some "cult of terror." Instead, it is

the realization that in order to be effective and ulti-mately successful, any revolutionary movement within advanced capitalist nations must develop the broadest possible range of thinking/action by which to confront the state. This should be conceived not as an array of component forms of struggle, but as a continuum of activity stretching from petitions/letter writing and so forth through mass mobilizations/demonstrations onward into the arena of armed self-defense, and still onward through the realm of "offensive" military oper-ations (e.g., elimination of critical state facilities, tar-geting of key individuals within the governmental cor-porate apparatus, etc.). All this must be apprehended as a holism, as an internally consistent liberatory process applicable at this generally formulated level to the late capitalist context no less than to the Third World. From the basis of this fundamental understand-ing and, it may be asserted, *only* from this basis can a viable liberatory praxis for North America emerge.[42]

I am arguing that on the basis of the recognition of the inter-relatedness implied in such a continuum, in such a spectrum of activity, we begin to seriously recognize our current short-comings for what they are: dogma that must be replaced by honest theory, a reactionary rote-like protest that has dis-placed honest practice. I am arguing that we recognize, as Barbara Deming has, that:

There is a sense even in which we do share the same faith. When we define the kind of world we want to bring into being, our vision and theirs too is of a world in which no person exploits another, abuses, dominates another—in short, a nonviolent world. We differ about how to bring this world into being: and that's a very real difference. But we are in the same struggle and we need each other. We need to take strength from each other, and we need to learn from each other. . . . I think it is very important that we not be too sure that they have all the learning to do, and we have all the teaching. It seems obvious to us right now that the methods they are sometimes willing to use are inconsistent with the vision we both hold of the new world. It is just possible—as we pursue that vision—that we are in some way inconsistent, too, for we have been in the past.[43]

I am suggesting that we must recognize a symbiosis between our struggles, that when any of us are stronger, all of us are stronger; when any of us are weaker, all of us are weaker. I am suggesting that we develop a genuine praxis, and here i am using praxis, as Churchill did, to mean action consciously and intentionally guided by theory while simultaneously guiding the evolution of theoretical elaboration.[44] If we fail to do so, we abdicate our revolutionary responsibility and remain for the oppressed of this Earth nothing more than Her Majesty's Loyal Opposition.

Notes

1 Ward Churchill and Michael Ryan, *Pacifism as Pathology* (Oakland: PM Press, 2017).

2 Kelly Booth, "Nonviolence: The Way of Nature," *New Catalyst*, Vol. 1, No. 3 (March–April 1986) p. 3.

3 Ibid.

4 Rosalie Bertell, "Early War Crimes of World War III," in *A Case for Non-Violent Resistance* (Toronto: Cruise Missile Conversion Project, 1984) p. 23.

5 Anonymous, "Thoughts on Consolidation," *Notes from a New Afrikan POW Journal*, Vol. 7, p. 35.

6 Mao Tse-tung, "To Be Attacked by the Enemy Is a Good Thing Not a Bad Thing," May 26, 1939, online at https://www.marxists.org/reference/archive/mao/selected-works/volume-6/mswv6_32.htm..

7 Anonymous, "Nonviolent Solidarity with a Violent Struggle," in Women's Action for Peace/Alliance for Non-Violent Action, *Pornography, Rape, War: Making the Links* (Fall 1984) p. 33.

8   Ibid.

9   Churchill, *Pacifism as Pathology*, pp. 72–73.

10   Judy Costello, "Beyond Gandhi: An American Feminists Approach to Nonviolence," in Pam McAllister, ed., *Reweaving the Web of Life* (Philadelphia: New Society Publishers, 1982) pp. 179–80.

11   Rolling Thunder, cited in *The Vancouver Five: A Story of Struggle to Protect the Earth*, anonymous, undated, no page numbers.

12   Shanna Bakari, "On Concrete Solidarity," *Notes from a New Afrikan POW Journal*, Vol. 2, p. 33.

13   Henry David Thoreau, *On the Duty of Civil Disobedience* (Project Gutenberg EBook #71, 2004; updated 2011) p. 7, online at http://www.gutenberg.org/ebooks/71.

14   Ibid., p. 12.

15   Henry David Thoreau, "A Plea for Captain John Brown," October 30, 1859, online at http://thoreau.eserver.org/plea2.html.

16   Ibid.

17   Martin Luther King, "Conscience and the Vietnam War," in *Conscience and Social Change* (Toronto: CBC Productions, The Massey Lectures, 1967) p. 18.

18   Martin Luther King, "Youth and Social Action," in *Conscience and Social Change*, p. 23.

19   Martin Luther King, "Conscience and the Vietnam War," p. 32.

20   Doug Man, "The Movement," *New Catalyst*, Vol. 1, No. 8 (March/April 1986) p. 17.

21   Pat James, "Physical Resistance to Attack: The Pacifist's Dilemma, The Feminists Hope," in *Reweaving the Web of Life*, p. 389.

22   Frantz Fanon, *The Wretched of the Earth* (New York: Evergreen Black Cat Edition, 1968) p. 35.

23   Nelson Mandela, *It Is Our Duty to Resist* (Hartford, Connecticut: Worldview Forum, 1986) p. 6.

24   Ibid., p. 22.

25   George Lakey, *A Manifesto for Nonviolent Revolution* (Philadelphia: Movement for a New Society Publishers, 1976) p. 25.

26   Quoted in Fanon, *Wretched of the Earth*, p. 103.

27   Ibid., p. 106.

28   Ward Churchill and Winona La Duke, "Radioactive Colonization and the Native American," *Socialist Review*, Vol. 15, No. 3 (Spring 1986) p. 77.

29   Ibid., p. 118. For Churchill's use of the terms indigenist and indigenism, see his "On Support of the Indian Resistance in Nicaragua: A Statement of Position and Principle," *Akwesasne Notes*, Vol. 18, No. 5 (Autumn 1986).

30   "Anarchafilmmaker: An Interview with Lizzie Borden," *Kick It Over*, No. 18 (Spring 1987) p. 3n.

31   Malcolm X, *Malcolm X Talks to Young People* (New York: Pathfinder Press, 1965) p. 4.

32   Ibid., p. 15.

33   Philip S. Foner, ed., *The Black Panthers Speak* (Philadelphia: J.B. Lippincott, 1970) p. 3.

34   Ibid., p. 85.

35   Omali Yeshitela, *The Struggle for Bread, Peace, and Black Power* (Oakland: Burning Spear, 1981) p. 65.

36   Foner, *The Black Panthers Speak*, p. 55.

37   Ibid., p. 229.

38   Ibid., p. 237.

39   Anonymous, *Redefining Violence*, pamphlet, no place or publisher (April 5, 1975) p. 72.

40   James, "Physical Resistance to Attack," p. 389.

41   Anonymous, *Women's Encampment for a Future of Peace and Justice: Resource Handbook*, Seneca Army Depot Peace Camp (Summer 1983) p. 23.

42   Churchill, *Pacifism as Pathology*, pp. 104–5.

43   Barbara Demming, *On Anger*, pamphlet reprinted from *Liberation* (Palo Alto, CA: Institute for the Study of Nonviolence, no date) p. 2.

44   Churchill, *Pacifism as Pathology*, p. 99.

Index

"Passim" (literally "scattered") indicates intermittent discussion of a topic over a cluster of pages.

About the Authors

Ward Churchill was, until moving to Atlanta in 2012, a member of the leadership council of Colorado AIM. He is a life member of Vietnam Veterans Against the War and currently a member of the elders council of the original Rainbow Coalition, founded by Chicago Black Panther leader Fred Hampton in 1969. Now retired, Churchill was professor of American Indian Studies and chair of the Department of Ethnic Studies until 2005, when he became the focus of a major academic freedom case. Among his two dozen books are *Agents of Repression* and *The COINTELPRO Papers* (1990, 2002), both coauthored with Jim Vander Wall, as well as *A Little Matter of Genocide* (1997), *Acts of Rebellion* (2003), and *Wielding Words like Weapons* (2017).

Michael Ryan is a Montréal-based translator and copy editor. From the mid-1970s to the mid-1990s, Ryan was active in Montréal's Marxist and antiauthoritarian left. (He insists that the two are not mutually exclusive.) Ryan continues to believe that if we want true social change we're going to have to kick it over.

Ed Mead is a former political prisoner who was arrested for his participation in actions carried out by the George Jackson Brigade in the Pacific Northwest during the 1970s. He spent eighteen years in prison and, while at Washington's Walla Walla State Correctional Facility, helped found Men Against Sexism, thereby halting prisoner-on-prisoner rape while he was confined there. Also a cofounder of *Prison Legal News*, his memoir *Lumpen* was published in 2015.

Dylan Rodríguez is professor and chair of the Department of Ethnic Studies at the University of California, Riverside. He is the author of two books: *Forced Passages: Imprisoned Radical Intellectuals and the U.S. Prison Regime* (2006) and *Suspended Apocalypse: White Supremacy, Genocide, and the Filipino Condition* (2009). His current thinking, writing, and teaching focus on how regimes of social liquidation, cultural extermination, physiological evisceration, and racist terror become normalized features of everyday life in the "post–civil rights" and "postracial" moments.

ABOUT PM PRESS

PM Press was founded at the end of 2007 by a small collection of folks with decades of publishing, media, and organizing experience. PM Press co-conspirators have published and distributed hundreds of books, pamphlets, CDs, and DVDs. Members of PM have founded enduring book fairs, spearheaded victorious tenant organizing campaigns, and worked closely with bookstores, academic conferences, and even rock bands to deliver political and challenging ideas to all walks of life. We're old enough to know what we're doing and young enough to know what's at stake.

We seek to create radical and stimulating fiction and non-fiction books, pamphlets, T-shirts, visual and audio materials to entertain, educate, and inspire you. We aim to distribute these through every available channel with every available technology—whether that means you are seeing anarchist classics at our bookfair stalls, reading our latest vegan cookbook at the café, downloading geeky fiction e-books, or digging new music and timely videos from our website.

PM Press is always on the lookout for talented and skilled volunteers, artists, activists, and writers to work with. If you have a great idea for a project or can contribute in some way, please get in touch.

PM Press
PO Box 23912
Oakland, CA 94623
www.pmpress.org

FRIENDS OF PM PRESS

These are indisputably momentous times—the
financial system is melting down globally and
the Empire is stumbling. Now more than ever
there is a vital need for radical ideas.

In the years since its founding—and on a
mere shoestring—PM Press has risen to the formidable challenge
of publishing and distributing knowledge and entertainment for the
struggles ahead. With over 300 releases to date, we have published an
impressive and stimulating array of literature, art, music, politics, and
culture. Using every available medium, we've succeeded in connecting
those hungry for ideas and information to those putting them into
practice.

Friends of PM allows you to directly help impact, amplify, and revitalize
the discourse and actions of radical writers, filmmakers, and artists. It
provides us with a stable foundation from which we can build upon our
early successes and provides a much-needed subsidy for the materials
that can't necessarily pay their own way. You can help make that
happen—and receive every new title automatically delivered to your
door once a month—by joining as a Friend of PM Press. And, we'll throw
in a free T-shirt when you sign up.

Here are your options:

- **$30 a month** Get all books and pamphlets plus 50% discount on all
  webstore purchases

- **$40 a month** Get all PM Press releases (including CDs and DVDs)
  plus 50% discount on all webstore purchases

- **$100 a month** Superstar—Everything plus PM merchandise, free
  downloads, and 50% discount on all webstore purchases

For those who can't afford $30 or more a month, we're introducing
Sustainer Rates at $15, $10 and $5. Sustainers get a free PM Press
T-shirt and a 50% discount on all purchases from our website.

Your Visa or Mastercard will be billed once a month, until you tell us to
stop. Or until our efforts succeed in bringing the revolution around. Or
the financial meltdown of Capital makes plastic redundant. Whichever
comes first.

Wielding Words like Weapons: Selected Essays in Indigenism, 1995–2005

Ward Churchill with a Foreword by Barbara Alice Mann

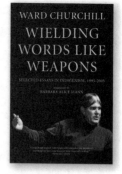

ISBN: 978-1-62963-101-1
$27.95   616 pages

Wielding Words like Weapons is a collection of acclaimed American Indian Movement activist-intellectual Ward Churchill's essays in indigenism, selected from material written during the decade 1995–2005. Beginning with a foreword by Seneca historian Barbara Alice Mann describing sustained efforts by police and intelligence agencies as well as university administrators and other academic adversaries to discredit or otherwise "neutralize" both the man and his work, the book includes material illustrating the range of formats Churchill has adopted in stating his case, from sharply framed book reviews and review essays, to equally pointed polemics and op-eds, to formal essays designed to reach both scholarly and popular audiences.

The items selected, several of them previously unpublished, also reflect the broad range of topics addressed in Churchill's scholarship, from the fallacies of archeological/anthropological orthodoxy like the Bering Strait migration hypothesis and the insistence of "cannibalogists" that American Indians were traditionally maneaters, to cinematic degradations of native people by Hollywood, the historical and ongoing genocide of North America's native peoples, questions of American Indian identity, and the systematic distortion of political and legal history by reactionary scholars as a means of denying the realities of U.S.-Indian relations. Also included are both the initial "stream-of-consciousness" version of Churchill's famous—or notorious—"little Eichmanns" opinion piece analyzing the causes of the attacks on 9/11, as well as the counterpart essay in which his argument was fully developed, which garnered honorable mention for the 2004 Gustavus Myers Award for best writing on human rights.

"Compellingly original, with the powerful eloquence and breadth of knowledge we have come to expect from Churchill's writing."
—Howard Zinn

"This is insurgent intellectual work—breaking new ground, forging new paths, engaging us in critical resistance."
—bell hooks

From a Native Son: Selected Essays in Indigenism, 1985–1995, Second Edition

Ward Churchill with an Introduction by Howard Zinn

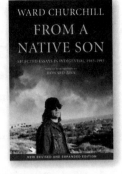

ISBN: 978-1-62963-108-0
$24.95   608 pages

From a Native Son was the first volume of acclaimed American Indian Movement activist-intellectual Ward Churchill's essays in indigenism, selected from material written during the decade 1985–1995. Presented here in a newly revised edition that includes four additional pieces, three of them previously unpublished, the book illuminates Churchill's early development of the themes with which he has, in the words of Noam Chomsky, "carved out a special place for himself in defending the rights of oppressed people, and exposing the dark side of past and current history, often forgotten, marginalized, or suppressed."

Topics addressed include the European conquest and colonization of the Americas, including the genocidal record of Christopher Columbus, the systematic "clearing" and resettlement of American Indian territories by the United States and its antecedents, academic subterfuges designed to deny or disguise the extent of Indian land rights, radioactive contamination of Indian reservations by energy corporations, government-sponsored death squads used to "neutralize" the native struggle on the Pine Ridge Reservation during the mid-1970s, the ongoing dehumanization of American Indians in literature, cinema, and by their portrayal as sports team mascots, issues of Indian identity and the expropriation of indigenous spiritual traditions, the negative effects of "postmodernism" upon understandings of contemporary circumstances of native people, the false promise of marxism in terms of indigenous liberation, and what, from an indigenist standpoint, the genuine decolonization of North America might look like. Of particular interest is Churchill's inclusion in the new version of his 1986 "On Support of the Indian Resistance in Nicaragua" concerning the Indian/Sandinista conflict along the Atlantic Coast of Nicaragua, an item which should go far in dispelling recent confusion about his thinking and actions in that regard.

"Ward Churchill points out the traditional Indian views more than anyone else."
—John Ross Jr., former principal chief United Keetoowah Band of Cherokee Indians

Creating a Movement with Teeth: A Documentary History of the George Jackson Brigade

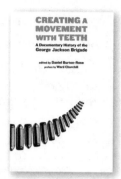

Edited by Daniel Burton-Rose
with a preface by Ward Churchill

ISBN: 978-1-60486-223-2
$24.95   320 pages

Bursting into existence in the Pacific Northwest in 1975, the George Jackson Brigade claimed 14 pipe bombings against corporate and state targets, as many bank robberies, and the daring rescue of a jailed member. Combining veterans of the prisoners', women's, gay, and black liberation movements, this organization was also ideologically diverse, consisting of both communists and anarchists. Concomitant with the Brigade's extensive armed work were prolific public communications. In more than a dozen communiqués and a substantial political statement, they sought to explain their intentions to the public while defying the law enforcement agencies that pursued them.

Collected in one volume for the first time, *Creating a Movement with Teeth* makes available this body of propaganda and mediations on praxis. In addition, the collection assembles corporate media profiles of the organization's members and alternative press articles in which partisans thrash out the heated debates sparked in the progressive community by the eruption of an armed group in their midst. *Creating a Movement with Teeth* illuminates a forgotten chapter of the radical social movements of the 1970s in which diverse interests combined forces in a potent rejection of business as usual in the United States.

"Creating a Movement with Teeth *is an important contribution to the growing body of literature on armed struggle in the 1970s. It gets us closer to knowing not only how pervasive militant challenges to the system were, but also the issues and contexts that shaped such strategies. Through documents by and about the George Jackson Brigade, as well as the introduction by Daniel Burton-Rose, this book sheds light on events that have until now been far too obscured.*"
—Dan Berger, author of *Outlaws of America: The Weather Underground and the Politics of Solidarity*; editor of *The Hidden 1970s: Histories of Radicalism*.

Look for Me in the Whirlwind: From the Panther 21 to 21st-Century Revolutions

Sekou Odinga, Dhoruba Bin Wahad, Jamal Joseph
Edited by Matt Meyer & dequi kioni-sadiki with a Foreword by Imam Jamil Al-Amin, and an Afterword by Mumia Abu-Jamal

ISBN: 978-1-62963-389-3
$24.95   448 pages

In the tumultuous year of 1969, amid music festivals and moon landings, assassinations and million-person antiwar mobilizations, twenty-one members of the militant New York branch of the Black Panther Party (BPP) were rounded up and indicted on multiple charges of violent acts and conspiracies. They were charged with plans to blow up a variety of sites—from a police station in Manhattan to the Queens offices of the Board of Education and the Bronx Botanical Gardens. Though some among the New York Panther 21 (NY 21) had hardly even met one another, the group was gathered together as an obvious attempt by the FBI, in cooperation with city and state authorities, to discredit, disrupt, and destroy the organization which was attracting so many young people across the world. In the ensuing preparation for a trial that would become the longest and most expensive in New York's history at the time, information came out about the FBI's illegal Counterintelligence Program (COINTELPRO), as members of the BPP were assassinated, forced into exile, framed, and set against each other.

In the case of the NY 21, splits between the California-based Huey Newton and Bobby Seale, and the New York–based Panthers, who had a more internationalist and clandestine approach, became hostile and murderous. At the same time, solidarity for the 21 extended well beyond predictable Black Liberation circles, including a cocktail party fundraiser hosted by Leonard Bernstein which was infamously derided in mainstream media reports. Support for the 21 also included publication of the collective autobiography *Look for Me in the Whirlwind*, which is reprinted for the first time in this volume.

The Red Army Faction, A Documentary History Volume 2: Dancing with Imperialism

Edited by J. Smith and André Moncourt with an Introduction by Ward Churchill

ISBN: 978-1-60486-030-6
$26.95   480 pages

The long-awaited *Volume 2* of the first-ever English-language study of the Red Army Faction—West Germany's most notorious urban guerillas—covers the period immediately following the organization's near-total decimation in 1977. This work includes the details of the guerilla's operations, and its communiqués and texts, from 1978 up until the 1984 offensive.

This was a period of regrouping and reorientation for the RAF, with its previous focus on freeing its prisoners replaced by an anti-NATO orientation. This was in response to the emergence of a new radical youth movement in the Federal Republic, the Autonomen, and an attempt to renew its ties to the radical left. The possibilities and perils of an armed underground organization relating to the broader movement are examined, and the RAF's approach is contrasted to the more fluid and flexible practice of the Revolutionary Cells. At the same time, the history of the 2nd of June Movement (2JM), an eclectic guerilla group with its roots in West Berlin, is also evaluated, especially in light of the split that led to some 2JM members officially disbanding the organization and rallying to the RAF. Finally, the RAF's relationship to the East German Stasi is examined, as is the abortive attempt by West Germany's liberal intelligentsia to defuse the armed struggle during Gerhard Baum's tenure as Minister of the Interior.

Dancing with Imperialism will be required reading for students of the First World guerilla, those with interest in the history of European protest movements, and all who wish to understand the challenges of revolutionary struggle.